insight text guide

Robert Beardwood

I'm Not Scared

Niccolò Ammaniti

First published in 2004. Reprinted 2010, 2012, 2013, 2015, 2016, 2020, 2021, 2024.

Insight Publications Pty Ltd
3/350 Charman Road
Cheltenham VIC 3192
Australia
Tel: +61 3 8571 4950
Email: books@insightpublications.com.au

www.insightpublications.com.au

National Library of Australia Cataloguing-in-Publication entry:
Beardwood, Robert, 1966-.
Insight text guide: I'm Not Scared – Niccolo Ammaniti.
ISBN 9781920693633
1. Ammaniti, Niccolo, 1966-. Io non ho paura. I. Title.
(Series: Insight text guide).
853.914

Other ISBNs:
9781925316230 (digital)

Cover design: The Modern Art Production Group

Printed by Markono Print Media Pte Ltd

contents

CHARACTER MAP

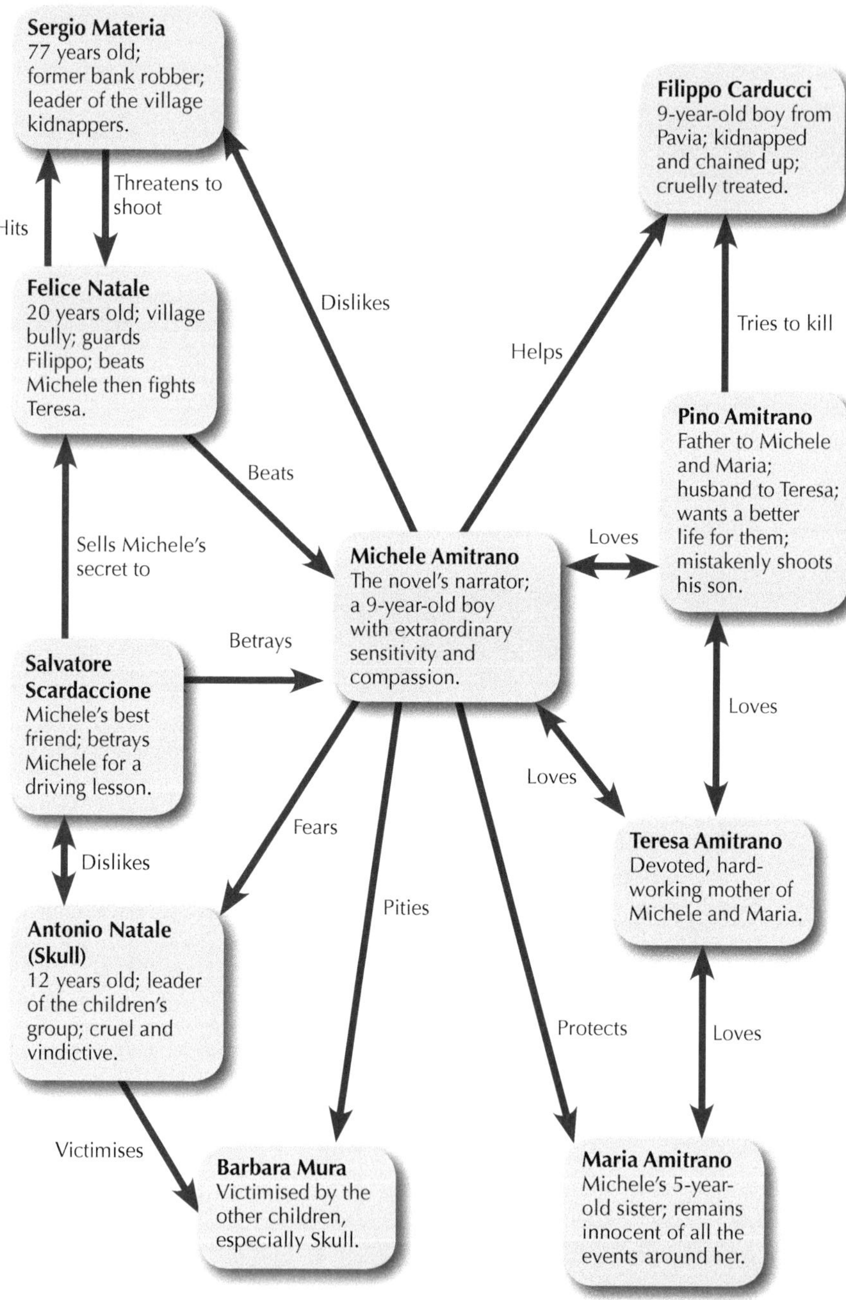

INTRODUCTION

Told from the simultaneously naive and discerning perspective of a nine-year-old boy named Michele, and set in the sun-scorched fields of southern Italy, *I'm Not Scared* is a thriller with a moral vision. It explores the complex, yet necessary obligations of morality – both for the individual and for society as a whole – and the paralysing grip that fear can exert on the human psyche.

On one level it is a coming-of-age story, in which a precipitous discovery propels Michele from childhood innocence into a world that requires difficult choices to be made and serious responsibilities to be borne. On another level, *I'm Not Scared* is a fable about the persistence and rewards of simple virtues: the loyalty and love of family and friends; the value of compassion for those who are suffering; an appreciation of the natural world in all its phases. It is when the adults of Acqua Traverse lose sight of these virtues, betraying the very values they have taught their children, that things go awry, threatening the existence of everything secure and pleasurable in their lives.

About Niccolò Ammaniti

The perfectly executed combination of an irresistible narrative drive and Michele's quirky, often comical narrative voice, of compelling characters and universal themes, have launched *I'm Not Scared* onto bestseller lists around the world. Born in Rome in 1966, Niccolò Ammaniti is a young author whose success with this novel follows a relatively modest start to his writing career. Prior to the 2001 Italian publication of *Io non ho paura* (more literally, 'I have no fear'), Ammaniti had published a collection of short stories and two other novels, and had been involved in film adaptations of his fiction. An interest in horror and the grotesque runs through his writing, and is evident again in *I'm Not Scared*. Ammaniti also worked on the screenplay for the film version of the novel, which began screening in Australian cinemas in 2004.

BACKGROUND & CONTEXT

Places in Italy

Acqua Traverse is a fictional place in Italy. Although its name suggests there is 'water across' the region, the novel's landscape is parched and water has to be trucked in each fortnight. Lucignano, the closest main town where the characters shop, is a real town in southern Tuscany, with a history dating back to medieval times. This combination of real and fictional places allows Ammaniti to fuse elements of social realism – especially through his evocative descriptions of the countryside, the poverty of the village and the rigours of the summer – with elements of fable and fairytale.

The Carducci family lives in Pavia, which is south of Milan in the northern region of Italy known as Lombardy (in the news report, Giovanni Carducci is referred to as 'the Lombard businessman', p.85). Thus, the Carduccis live in Italy's relatively prosperous north, while the Amitranos live in the south, poor and apparently unable to improve the quality of their lives, at least by legitimate means. As Michele reflects, 'the North was rich and the South was poor. And we were poor' (p.32). The text is certainly sympathetic to the Amitranos' sense of an unfair gap in Italian society between rich and poor, but by narrating events from Michele's perspective continually questions the adults' moral judgments as they attempt to bridge this social divide.

The other important Italian city referred to is Rome, which is where Sergio comes from, and where Salvatore's father, the Avvocato Emilio Scardaccione, is 'a big shot' (p.3). As the centre of Italian government, Rome represents the larger forces of the world, seemingly remote from the isolated village of Acqua Traverse but also able to reach into it through the influence of these two characters. Intriguingly, the Avvocato works on the side of the law (Michele refers to him as 'the lawyer' on p.155), whereas Sergio appears to be a career criminal. In the events of the narrative, though, both work together as criminals, suggesting that those who are powerful attend more to their own interests than to the interests of society or of the law.

Italian terms

From time to time in this text the translator, Jonathan Hunt, leaves a few words in the original Italian, allowing the narrative to retain something of its local colour and distinctive cultural identity. However, this can leave English-speaking readers (at least, those who don't speak Italian) unsure of what is actually being said at a particular point; below are translations of some of these Italian terms and phrases.

- The title, *Io non ho paura*, translates literally as 'I have no fear', although in informal contexts – such as those portrayed in the text – the translation 'I'm not scared' is accurate.
- Salvatore's father is 'the Avvocato Emilio Scardaccione' (p.3): 'Avvocato' means 'solicitor'.
- Michele hears an aria from Verdi's opera *La Traviata* on the radio as his mother smacks him for returning home late (p.79); the line he remembers is: *'Croce. Croce e delizia. Delizia al cor'*. This translates in the operatic context as 'agony and ecstasy', or in more prosaic terms, 'pain and delight', with 'Croce' meaning 'cross to bear'. The aria thus provides an ironic commentary on the action, since Teresa is finding Michele to be a source of both pain and delight in her life.
- Barbara Mura sings "*O bella ciao*!" (p.96): this means 'O beautiful day' – a form of greeting to the morning.

GENRE, STRUCTURE & LANGUAGE

Structure

The novel is divided into ten chapters, which are neither numbered nor titled. Each of the first seven chapters corresponds to a single day, typically beginning with Michele waking and ending with him falling asleep. In this way, a relatively ordered, predictable existence is reflected in the structure of the narrative. The ordering of time signifies the continuity of other kinds of order, such as the integrity of families, community life and the moral order that governs human interaction. However, the seventh chapter begins with the line 'Everything was in disarray' (p.159), indicating that this existence is under threat.

The eighth chapter (pp.168–73) begins with 'And everything stopped', signalling the end of any kind of certainty about what will happen next. The days continue to pass, but uneventfully and undifferentiated. This marks the suspension of known structures, including those of the family and of the moral order. In the text, the moral order includes being true to one's promises, being compassionate towards those who are less fortunate, and being able to trust one's parents unquestioningly. Such structures make sense of existence, providing explanations of causes and effects. However, from chapter 8, such structures are (at least for Michele) no longer a 'given' of existence; even questions are suspended.

The feeling of taut stillness in the eighth chapter is partially relieved by the restoration of the friendship between Michele and Salvatore and then, in the following chapter (pp.174–87), by the breaking of the storm and the information that Filippo is still alive. In the tenth and final chapter, the inversion of any kind of natural order in Michele's life is reflected by his waking not in the morning (as in the earlier chapters) but in the middle of the night.

Language: images of cruelty and capture

Although the narrative is apparently simply told, it is in fact intricately crafted. Many images introduced early in the narrative – innocuous enough at first – anticipate later incidents of much greater weight and significance.

Images of cruelty and capture introduce these topics as central concerns for the text from the beginning. At Michele's suggestion, a hen is placed in a bag to be fed to Melichetti's pigs, but is later impaled on a stick; this is merely the first of many images of entrapment and cruelty towards animals. Italo Natale's dogs are kept 'locked up ... summer and winter, behind wire netting' (p.66), and their howling one night makes Michele look 'towards the hill' (p.66), thinking of the boy whose freedom, like that of the dogs, has been taken away from him.

Another image that puts the adults' treatment of Filippo in a chilling light is that of a cat playing with lizards, dismembering them until they become bored, when they leave their prey to a long, slow death (p.184). This sense of cruelty being for amusement, rather than survival, and of indifference to the suffering of another creature, is inconsistent with most people's conception of ethical behaviour. Yet Michele makes a clear link between this image and his own father's treatment of Filippo.

Michele's imagination also furnishes images of entrapment, mostly through the figures of the Wicked Witch who catches Pierino Pierone and 'tied him up in a sack' (p.90) and the ogre who has 'a sack full of children' (p.114). These images provide a commentary on Filippo's capture and entrapment, suggesting that his experience is less an isolated case than a symptom of a society regulated not by pity and compassion but by fear, greed and cruelty.

Images that gain significance through repetition

Some incidents referred to early in the narrative are later reprised, or echoed, thus giving them much greater emotional impact. These include Teresa giving Felice 'a thrashing' (p.77) after Felice had pulled the ears of Michele and Skull. This incident is echoed when Teresa fights Felice over his treatment of Michele at the abandoned house; on this occasion there is much more at stake, and Felice is a much more threatening figure (pp.151–2). Additionally, the fact that Felice had pulled at the boys' ears anticipates the threat that he will cut off one or both of Filippo's ears (p.86).

When Michele wonders about the boy's identity, he remembers his father telling him that 'Monsters don't exist ... It's men you should be afraid of' (p.49). It seems to be sensible, father-to-son advice, but Michele does not imagine that it is his own father, in fact, of whom he needs to be afraid. Michele remembers his father's words on the last afternoon (p.184), and their real significance becomes apparent to him.

Q There are several images of falling in the narrative. What are they, and how do they relate to Michele's feelings of fear and vulnerability?

Style: the use of humour

the narrative tension steadily increases throughout the novel – which follows the overall form of a thriller – but it is leavened by humour. Elements of the horror genre in this narrative are generally comic in their effect, not least because Michele realises that the fantastical creatures inhabiting his imagination – ogres, witches, and so on – do not actually exist. Also, these horror elements are usually so exaggerated that they tend to relieve narrative tension rather than heighten it. When Michele imagines the boy in the hole to be dead, he envisages the corpse with 'worms coming out of his blue lips' and eyes 'like two hard-boiled eggs' (p.39). It is the exaggerated grotesqueness of this image, the incongruity of a person having hard-boiled eggs as eyeballs, that makes it partly horrific, and partly comic.

Similarly, when Salvatore tells the 'true story' (p.80) of a man's son brought back to life by a wizard, he describes in graphic detail the son's 'brains running out' (p.81). The story, initially tragic in tone, comes to seem so divorced from reality that the image is more comic than distressing. Salvatore's laconic, understated style further enhances this effect.

Humour also enters the text through references to bodily functions and excretions. The idea of boys urinating in unusual places invariably introduces a comic note, as when Michele's 'pee drummed on the tarpaulin of the truck' (p.87) or Sergio's son died 'with his dick sticking out of his pants' (p.118) after (apparently) relieving himself by the side of a road. Maria is always amused by stories 'with doo-doo in them' (p.90), and there are several such episodes in *I'm Not Scared*. Michele 'thrashed about in the shit' (p.47) after tipping over Filippo's bucket, and then at the end of the narrative he smears himself with the 'piss-soaked earth' around Melichetti's pigs to avoid provoking them (p.203) – only to slip 'in the dung' moments later (p.204).

Michele's unique world view

The most consistent source of humour, though, is Michele's innocent, idiosyncratic way of viewing the world and imagining how things operate in it. Even as he contemplates being unable to return to Filippo, and understands the serious danger that Filippo is in, he imagines his father passing on his apologies: "Michele can't come ... If he comes they'll kill you. He sends his regards" (p.162). It is a vision of a simple, decent action that is so inconsistent with reality that even Michele realises its incongruity.

At other times, Michele provides a whimsical image to explain his experience, frequently relieving the dramatic tension of his narrative in the process. For instance, when describing the knock to his head while fighting Felice, he explains that: 'A kettle started whistling in my head' (p.152).

Similarly, when Michele realises that Salvatore has betrayed him, he recalls his image of the Scardaccione sisters 'on the edge of the quicksands beavering away on their sewing machine and me sinking' (p.148), a poignant image of human indifference to suffering that is injected with a comic note by the idea of the women throwing honey drops at the sinking Michele. Again, this is a very significant, serious image of a vulnerable person sinking or having fallen and of those above being able to help but unwilling to do so – yet it is lightened with humour.

CHAPTER-BY-CHAPTER ANALYSIS

Epigraph

Ammaniti prefaces the narrative with a brief epigraph by the American novelist Jack London (1876–1916), who became famous for adventure and travel narratives such as *The Call of the Wild* (1903) and *White Fang* (1906). The importance of the epigraph lies in its image 'fallen into darkness', which anticipates not only Filippo's entrapment in a hole in the ground, but also Michele's 'fall' into a world of moral 'darkness' and even the fragmentation of the village community. This sense of uncertainty and confusion is hinted at in the epigraph's third sentence: 'And at the instant he knew, he ceased to know', which encapsulates Michele's bewilderment from the moment he comes to 'know' about Filippo's plight.

(Chapter 1) (pp.1–41)

Summary: *The six children of Acqua Traverse discover an abandoned farmhouse; Michele discovers what appears to be a dead boy in a concealed hole, but tells no-one.*

The novel opens on a summer's day in mid June 1978, in the vast wheat fields surrounding a tiny Italian village called Acqua Traverse. The six children of the village are in the midst of a race to the top of a hill; the narrative thus begins with action, only later filling in the details of the setting, the characters' names and attributes, and the circumstances that have led up to the race.

The narrative style is extremely simple, consistent with the world view of a nine-year-old, relatively uneducated country boy. However, many of these early descriptions of characters and landscapes are loaded with meaning, anticipating later events. The intensity of the summer heat 'wasn't normal', setting the scene for a series of abnormal occurrences in the characters' lives; the adults 'shut themselves up indoors with the blinds drawn', suggesting that they are self-absorbed, unwilling to see things as they really are (p.2). Even Maria's fall, which causes her to 'disappear, swallowed up by the wheat' (p.1), prefigures Michele's discovery of the boy in the hole later in the chapter.

The children are introduced

Michele's brief introductions of each of the children also demonstrate Ammaniti's skill in using images that convey meaning on more than one level. Michele compares Maria's devotion to himself with that of 'a little mongrel rescued from a dog pound' (p.2), which also indicates something of Michele's sensitivity and compassion for others, including animals. His characterisation of his best friend, Salvatore, as 'a loner' (p.3) establishes an attribute that manifests negatively later in the narrative, when Salvatore's self-interest outweighs his loyalty to his friend. The leader of the group, Antonio Natale, is 'known as Skull' (p.3), a nickname that suggests emotional hardness. This quality is certainly possessed by Skull, and is especially evident in his cruelty towards Barbara, but becomes even more pronounced in the character of Skull's brother, Felice (introduced in Chapter 4).

Michele expresses the least affection or admiration for Barbara Mura, which is important because despite his dislike of her he nevertheless acts kindly towards her. Michele's refusal to treat people differently according to whether he likes or dislikes them becomes very apparent through his relationship with Barbara; initially, though, he thinks of her as 'like a demented sow' (p.4), someone barely worthy of pity. Once again, the natural world is the source of imagery for Michele, establishing another central aspect of his personality.

The roles of animals

From the beginning of the narrative, it is clear that animals are intimately involved in the lives of these characters. The natural cycles of life and death are completely familiar to the children, to such an extent that Michele's idea of taking a hen to Melichetti's pigs to "see how they tear it apart" is regarded simply as a 'really good one' (p.8). In fact, this is a rare instance of Michele's cruelty to an animal, and he is revolted when he comes across the impaled hen on the top of the hill, covered with flies and dripping blood (p.15).

Melichetti

Melichetti is a minor character in the text, but he plays an important role in these early pages because his actions are at odds with what Michele and the other children say about him. Although he is clearly an eccentric old man who is incapable of looking after his farm, he demonstrates none of the hostility attributed to him by the children. On the contrary, Melichetti tolerates their presence and calmly dismisses their accusation that he fed his old dachshund to his (reputedly) vicious pigs. Melichetti even invites the children to help themselves to his water, which they do. Skull's opinion that 'Melichetti was a piece of shit' (p.11) thus reflects much more harshly on Skull than on the old man.

Here, the reader becomes aware of the need to read 'between the lines' of Michele's narrative, and not to take everything in the narrative at face value. Partly this is because Michele is strongly swayed by the opinions of others, such as Skull and Salvatore – though most of all, as we see later, by his father – and he has not yet reached the point of making independent judgments according to the actual deeds of others rather than simply what they say.

The abandoned farmhouse and the forfeit

Just as Michele's compassion is clear when he begrudgingly stops to help his sister, gently removing her shoe (p.5) and blowing on her leg (p.14), his desire to save others from pain or embarrassment is evident when he offers to 'do the forfeit' for Barbara. Skull's exploitation of Barbara's defencelessness can be seen partly as an abuse of power, and partly as an expression of burgeoning sexual interest. Previously he has forced Barbara to show her breasts to the others; on this occasion, though, he proposes that she expose her genitals. To Michele, this is too great an invasion of Barbara's privacy, so although Skull has excused him from having to 'do the forfeit' Michele uses the group's rules to force a second vote.

For a brief moment, Michele looks back at these events from the perspective of 'twenty-two years' later (p.19), the year 2000. Only in this first chapter does he refer to any time later than 1978, although an occasional remark in subsequent chapters, such as 'even now, as an adult' (p.113), causes a slight shift in the narrative perspective. At one point Michele reflects on an event that occurred 'ten years later' (p.24), then when the children return to their village Michele remarks that 'Nowadays Acqua Traverse is a district of Lucignano' (p.30). From this point onwards, though, only the events of the summer of 1978 are described, ensuring that the reader is entirely absorbed by the drama.

Michele's 'forfeit' is to cross the abandoned farmhouse, a difficult task because the floors, beneath which is a barn, have mostly rotted away. Michele is thus placed in a state of suspension over a drop of 'at least four metres' (p.23). At one point he is 'paralysed in the doorway', yet knows he must continue (p.24). The task, then, is physically dangerous, but its psychological challenge is perhaps more significant.

Key point

Michele recalls the later episode of being stuck on a chairlift above a ski run, in which his physical predicament is exacerbated by his absolute solitude. The anecdote draws attention to the way in which Michele's forfeit isolates him from the others and forces him to make difficult decisions on his own, moment by moment. This is precisely the situation – of being suspended from normal life and the comfort of others' support – that his imminent discovery will place him in for the remainder of the narrative.

Michele safely crosses the rooms, but on leaving the house he discovers a concealed hole, inside of which is the body, seemingly a corpse, of a boy. The 'terrible stink of shit' (p.27) is a clue that the boy is still alive, and signals that he has been held in degrading circumstances. Even though his utter stillness suggests that he is dead, Michele cannot help but wonder if the boy is alive, a thought that returns to him later that night (p.39) and motivates his descent into the hole the following morning (p.46). Michele says nothing of his discovery, clinging to his secret as a precious object, and the children return home without further incident.

Acqua Traverse

The children's return to their village provides the narrative with its first opportunity to reflect on the social and material circumstances of the characters. The village is extremely isolated, a 'place forgotten by God and man', which depends on 'a tanker once a fortnight' for water (p.31). It contains only five houses, of which four are very simple, 'drab little houses'; Salvatore's house is the only one of substance, reflecting the relative affluence of the Scardacciones (p.31).

This narrative interest in social status is reinforced when the village is placed in a larger, national context: 'the North was rich and the South was poor. And we were poor' (p.32). Michele is fascinated by the idea of the North, since it represents wealth and escape from the hardships of life. It is also a place Michele knows nothing about, making it possible for him to project his fantasies for his future life onto it. The idea of the economic divide between the North and the South recurs later in the narrative, in the form of the wealthy family from Pavia which the adults of Acqua Traverse hold to ransom.

Pino and Teresa

The scene in which Michele and Maria prepare to have supper with their parents is the only one in which the family is contentedly together in the whole novel. Michele and Maria are especially pleased to see their father, Pino, who is mostly away travelling in his truck, and who relates warmly and easily to his children. This is a side of Pino's personality that is rarely displayed in the remainder of the narrative. He arm-wrestles Michele, whom he chides for being "weaker than a gnat" (p.35) before allowing his son, with Maria's assistance, to defeat him. Then, to settle the dispute over who will collect the water, he proposes a game of 'soldier's draw' in which he is an equal – and unlucky – participant. Pino performs the task in good humour, calling it "a dangerous mission" (p.37), showing that he is true to his word.

Pino's 'present' is something of an anticlimax, but Michele's initial pleasure in seeing the plastic gondola suggests how little in the way of material objects the family possesses. On the other hand, the joy they have in each other's company and the way they generate interest and amusement simply through conversation demonstrates a different kind of 'wealth', generated by coherent and stable family bonds. It is this kind of wealth that the actions of the village adults place under threat, as if they barely recognise or value its existence.

Lazarus, ogres, and the boy in the hole

Michele's nightmare and ensuing thoughts about the boy in the hole show how active his imaginative life is. Images from the Bible (Jesus raising Lazarus from the dead) merge with figures from fairytales (ogres) and scenes from horror films, and all seem as real as the oppressive heat or the sounds of his father snoring in the next room. The image of the impaled hen re-enters Michele's mind as he imagines his dead grandmother 'sitting at the table with the boy' (p.40). To such an imagination almost anything seems possible, and in many ways it is the force of Michele's imagination that drives the narrative forwards.

Q What is the significance of Pino's choice of a gondola as a gift for the family? Is this related to Michele's desire for his father to take them 'to the seaside for a swim' (p.41)?

(Chapter 2) (pp.42–56)

Summary: *Michele secretly returns to the hole and climbs into it; the boy sits up, and Michele flees; Pino is furious with Michele for arriving home late and filthy.*

The next day, Michele returns to the hole without telling anyone where he is going. He notices the birds and animals of the fields – magpies, a hawk, a hare – while also preparing himself mentally for the presence of witches or an ogre at the abandoned house. To fortify his courage, he thinks of a fictional character, 'Tiger Jack, Tex Willer's Indian buddy' (p.44); the act of pretending that he is 'Tiger's Italian son' helps Michele to overcome his fears.

Michele is not so much frightened as repulsed by the abject state of the body lying motionless, naked and filthy at the bottom of the hole. Yet Michele is also fascinated, tantalised by the possibility that the boy is still alive. Lowering himself into the hole, Michele sees just how cruelly the boy has been treated: he seems to have been starved of food, is unwashed and chained 'to a buried ring' (p.47). An open wound appears to be infected and the boy's excrement is everywhere, including on his own body. Michele thinks that 'There was nothing human about him any more' (p.45), which also suggests that the boy's captors lack some basic human qualities.

When Michele lifts the blanket that covers the boy's legs, one leg moves and then the boy sits up. Even at this point, Michele thinks of him more as a corpse than a living person: 'The dead boy started screaming too' (p.47). It is like a scene from a schlock-horror film, but the reader's knowledge that the boy is really alive and has been cruelly treated makes it full of pathos, too.

"It's men you should be afraid of, not monsters"

Michele's stimulated imagination arrives at an explanation for the boy's existence: he is a werewolf, chained up 'because he was dangerous' (p.48). At this point, though, Michele remembers his father telling him that monsters do not actually exist and that in fact it is "men you should be afraid of" (p.49). Michele must now confront and recognise the difference between what is imaginary and what is real.

Michele tries to tell his father about the boy in the hole, but instead is scolded for returning home so late and for being covered in excrement. Pino's anger at this point gives the first indication that he is capable of real aggression towards his son. Rather than express any concern for his son's well-being, Pino simply orders Michele to leave the house.

The carob tree

Michele goes to the carob tree near the stream; this tree and the area around it provide a space of refuge for the village children, a place where adults do not come. Michele climbs the tree, giving him a vantage point from which to look out over the surrounding fields, and which also affords a degree of privacy and concealment. Maria, though, knows exactly where to find him, and the playful banter between the two siblings (p.52) shows how close they are to each other.

Michele is determined to make his family miss him, but Maria immediately thinks of having "the room to myself" and acquiring Michele's comics. This in turn makes Michele admit he is not quite ready to leave home. He is further tempted to return by the prospect of 'Purée and eggs' for supper (p.53); Michele's love of both these foods suggests that his mother has chosen them especially as a form of consolation.

Teresa's beauty

Pino is absent from the family's supper, which is eaten in silence. This scene forms a stark contrast to the previous evening's joyful family gathering, and is a first sign of the fragmentation of family bonds that the remainder of the narrative charts. Michele reflects on his mother's ceaseless household work, a life of apparent drudgery about which she never complains and which has not yet – at least in the eyes of her son – tarnished her beauty. She draws the admiring gazes of other men yet 'was no flirt' (p.55), establishing Teresa as an embodiment not simply of physical beauty but of moral purity as well.

Witches and gypsies

As on the previous night, Michele falls asleep imagining witches, an ogre and gypsies at the abandoned house, taunting or torturing the boy. Of course they are fantastical creatures and Michele's thoughts are products of childhood stories, yet these monsters also reflect the truly aberrant, 'monstrous' nature of the crime that has been committed.

Q What does the story about 'a man who changed into a wolf' only to be shot by his son (p.48) suggest about father-son relationships?

How does it raise the possibility that the people we think we know best actually keep crucial aspects of themselves secret?

(Chapter 3) (pp.57–67)

Summary: *Michele suspects a connection between the boy and his own family.*

On the morning of the third day, Pietro Mura visits the Amitrano household. This introduces another of the village adults into the narrative, and the story of Pietro's abandoning his barber's business to become 'a small farmer' (p.58) reinforces the difficulty most inhabitants of Acqua Traverse experience in making a living.

Michele again tries to tell his father about the boy, but Pino refuses to listen, showing how inflexible he can be. Michele plays soccer with the other children, but is so preoccupied that he performs poorly. He sets off for the hill, not even confiding in Salvatore despite his friend's questions.

Returning to the hole, Michele has his first exchange of words with the boy, fetching him some water from a drum in the house. Michele's willingness to offer assistance is apparent, despite his anxiety about what 'the guardians of the hole' (p.60) might do to him. In the abandoned house he notices a saucepan, recently used and very similar to one from his own home, which now raises questions in Michele's mind, as well as the reader's, about his own family's involvement in the boy's capture.

The theory of the twin

Michele arrives home in time for lunch, escaping his parents' censure. Pino says that his 'friend', Sergio, will be staying with them, and later in the afternoon he drives off for the night, refusing to take his children or answer their questions about his activities.

Michele tries unsuccessfully to find the saucepan, further encouraging his imagination. When Maria's unwanted piece of meat from lunch also disappears, Michele connects these several unusual events together in another narrative. Now he wonders if the boy is his own twin, a crazy brother being raised in the hole. Michele thinks of Salvatore's brother, Nunzio, who 'wasn't a bad lunatic' but has nevertheless been institutionalised (pp.66–7). The question of normality and madness – and how distinct from each other they supposedly are – is thus raised; the remainder of the narrative suggests these two poles can become very close to each other.

An important feature of this scenario is that the reason Michele's (imaginary) twin brother is still alive is that Pino 'couldn't bring himself' to kill him (p.67). Michele continues to believe in his father's essential goodness, but his belief that Pino would not harm a boy who was 'his son after all' (p.67) ironically anticipates the final, tragic scene of the novel.

Q How does Ammaniti use humour to defuse the narrative tension in this chapter?

(Chapter 4) (pp.68–91)

Summary: *Michele sees Felice driving from the abandoned house; the boy talks about wash-bears; Sergio arrives and Michele discovers the adults' kidnapping plot.*

On the fourth day, Michele sees a (Fiat) 127 travelling from the abandoned house, a car that Michele knows belongs to Felice Natale. Felice is Skull's twenty-year-old brother and, to the children of Acqua Traverse, Felice is effectively the village bully. The fact that he seems to have come from the house makes Michele suspect a connection between Felice and the boy. It is clear that no good can be expected from Felice: his capacity for violence is indicated by his fondness for guns and for wearing 'combat jackets and camouflaged trousers' (p.70). Michele compares Felice to 'a poisonous weed' and describes his brown car as 'diarrhoea-coloured' (p.71); Michele feels certain that Felice is the person who has placed the boy in the hole.

Increasingly wary, Michele brings the boy cheese and water, both of which are rapidly consumed in silence. Eventually, Michele's attempts at conversation are rewarded by a few disjointed remarks about wash-bears, the bucket and the "lord of the worms" (pp.73–4). Although the flow of words and images is fragmented, the two boys have no trouble stringing together a conversation, an early sign of their compatibility, their shared skill at generating a narrative out of almost nothing. The boy thinks of himself as dead, just as Michele has thought of him more as a corpse than a living person; this really reflects the way the boy has been treated as a less-than-human object.

Disconcerted, and particularly unnerved by the boy's touch, Michele leaves, continuing to think over the possibility that the boy is dead. He arrives home late and is spanked by his mother. Since it follows Michele's recollection of his mother previously having given Felice 'a thrashing', this scene shows a tougher side to Teresa's character. Ammaniti injects this scene with humour through Michele's expressions – 'stronger than Superman', 'tan my backside' (p.78) – and through the opera music being played on the radio becoming a kind of accompaniment. Nevertheless, it is clear that discipline is very important in this family; boundaries of acceptable behaviour should be strictly observed. This only heightens the shock when, later in the chapter, Michel learns the details of the crime in which Pino and Teresa are involved.

The son who comes back from the dead

Michele spends some time with Salvatore, and their conversation contrasts intriguingly with Michele's earlier one with the boy in the hole. The two friends are obviously comfortable in each other's company but Michele elicits little in the way of information from Salvatore, whose remarks are generally brief and unrevealing. Michele's questions show how the boy's predicament continues to occupy his thoughts. Salvatore casts another light on the situation, though, with his story about a man who asks a wizard to bring his son back from the dead. The wish is granted, but the son is so grotesque that the father "got some petrol and set fire to him" (p.81).

This story complements Michele's earlier fantasy about his father being unable to kill Michele's twin brother, since in both cases the father's love for the son is evident but takes a corrupted form. The story about the son who shoots his werewolf-father (p.48) also forms part of this series. The question of father-son relationships thus gains increasing prominence in the narrative, in the approach to the most important scene in the novel.

Key scene

Michele learns of Filippo's identity and the kidnappers' plot

That night, Michele wakes to the sound of quarrelling in the kitchen, where the village adults and a stranger, an old man, are sitting around the table. The old man is Sergio Materia, a bank robber from Rome who abuses the others, including Pino and Felice, for their incompetency. Michele is shocked by Sergio's assumption of power, 'like the emperor' (p.84), and above all by the casual way in which Sergio rebukes Pino.

As Michele tries to creep past to go to the toilet, he sees what all the adults are focused on, a picture on the television of the boy. His name is Filippo Carducci, and the adults have kidnapped him in order to obtain a considerable ransom from his wealthy parents. His mother, Luisa, appeals to the kidnappers for compassion and to tell Filippo his parents love him. However, the adults disparage her plea, with Pino calling her "this cow" and threatening to cut off both of Filippo's ears (p.86). None of the adults show any sympathy for the Carduccis, not even for Filippo; the women seem unable to identify with Luisa Carducci, despite the very recognisable feelings she displays.

Michele is devastated by his own parents' involvement in such a cruel – and criminal – scheme, and clearly at this point he has no option other than to keep his knowledge of it a secret from them.

Michele now knows not only the boy's identity but also the connections between the boy, Felice, the other adults of the village and Michele's own parents. This scene thus has a central place in the novel – falling just before the halfway point of the narrative – in resolving a number of questions, yet raising many more. Questions about the boy's identity, how he has come to be in the hole, Felice's involvement and the probability that the saucepan in the abandoned house is in fact the one from Michele's own house are all resolved. More importantly, though, this scene transforms Michele's – and the reader's – perceptions of the adults' lives and characters. The narrative tension is not only sustained, but also increased, especially since Michele's knowledge of these affairs remains a secret from the adults.

'Papa was the bogeyman'

Michele's long-held beliefs in the existence of make-believe creatures such as witches and ogres do not immediately disappear, but he now makes a connection between these stories and worldly reality that was hitherto impossible for him to grasp: 'Papa was the bogeyman' (p.87). Michele is not unfamiliar with the natural cycles of birth and death, but such cruelty to children – in particular, the prospect, apparently readily contemplated by his father, that Filippo's ears will be cut off – has never been part of Michele's knowledge of the world. Previously it has been the stuff merely of fairytales, but now it is unambiguously a part of reality.

If Michele is shocked by this new perception he gains of the adults, and particularly of his father, Michele nevertheless retains the same moral certainties that have informed his entire childhood. Foremost amongst these is the central importance of the bond between mother and child. To Michele, the fact that the Carduccis are rich, while the Amitranos are poor, is irrelevant; what is most important is the obvious distress of Filippo's mother.

A bedtime story

Finally, Michele has to make up a story of his own in order to placate Maria, who has been woken by the noise and by Michele's urinating on the tarpaulin of their father's truck. Here, he mimics the function of fairytales, which keep children both obedient and also ignorant of the facts of the real world. Michele does not want Maria to know the truth since 'she might go out of her mind', so instead he tells her that the adults are playing bingo (p.88). Maria asks for a bedtime story, which makes Michele feel 'very honoured' (p.89), showing just how much value Michele attaches to stories and the telling of them.

However, on this occasion he cannot escape into the story quite as completely as he might like to; aspects of reality keep coming into his mind and entering the story. The wash-bears, 'the North' and the capture of an innocent boy all relate to the real story about Filippo rather than the mythical one about the Wicked Witch and Pierino Pierone. And reality is all the more pressing for Michele since only he is in a position to help.

Q What does Michele's description of Sergio's appearance suggest about the old man's character? Note the repetition of 'gold'/'golden' in three sentences on p.83.

Q Why do you think Michele feels that his father is effectively Sergio's 'servant' but his mother 'wasn't' (p.87)?

(Chapter 5) (pp.92–118)

Summary: *Michele worries about sleeping with Sergio; Felice guards Filippo, singing along with the radio; Michele gives Filippo his mother's message; Sergio talks about his sons.*

In the morning, Michele comes across Sergio shaving in the bathroom. Michele again emphasises Sergio's skinny physique, especially the 'two slender, hairless stilts' of his legs (p.92). It is as if something is lacking in Sergio, as if he is not quite healthy. As we learn more about Sergio, though, it seems that what is lacking is not so much physical as moral. Michele is adamant that he does not want to share his room with the old man, and pleads with his mother, almost giving away his secret when he says that Sergio will "take me away" (p.94). Teresa is suspicious but Michele runs off before she can extract more information from him.

Michele removes ticks from Togo

As previously, Michele retreats to the carob, the one truly safe place where adult restrictions and abuses do not operate. While he is hidden from view, Barbara arrives at the stream and submerges Togo the dog in the mud. When Michele confronts her she insists that she is bathing Togo in order to remove ticks, and however ineffective this treatment may be

Togo is certainly suffering from a severe tick infestation. It is Michele who acts efficaciously, painstakingly removing the parasites one by one with his fingers.

Key point

As always, Michele is attentive to any aspect of the natural world, closely observing the ticks' 'little black legs and their dark-brown stomachs' (p.97). What is most significant about this scene, though, is that Michele not only feels sympathy for creatures that suffer, but is willing and able to act to lessen that suffering.

Michele's compassion reinforces to Barbara his positive qualities, and after thanking him for doing the forfeit in her place she asks him to be her boyfriend. Michele is embarrassed, and declines – he is still not attracted to Barbara, and remains true to his feelings.

Felice sings and dances

Returning to the abandoned house, Michele finds Felice guarding Filippo, but behaving in an entirely unexpected way. Almost naked – wearing only underpants, army boots and 'the usual black bandanna round his neck' (p.100) – Felice dances and sings along to his car radio. The popular song, which Michele likes, features both male and female parts, so Felice sings the woman's role in falsetto and the man's 'in a deep voice'; Michele admits 'He was very good' (p.101).

Felice's unselfconsciously camp performance shows that there is much more to his character than Felice wants other people to know about. His 'tough guy' persona, then, is largely a constructed image, a form of self-defence rather than the 'real' Felice. Nevertheless, Michele is wary of the consequences if he is discovered, and returns to the village.

Skull and Salvatore

The game of 'one-two-three-star' (p.101) allows for the character of Skull to be further developed. He is always determined to win, willing to resort to cheating or physical violence in order to achieve what he wants. By representing the two Natale brothers as similar in their unpredictable and threatening demeanours, the narrative draws attention to the crucial role of family in shaping character traits. The earlier story about Skull and Felice's father, Italo, refusing to help a dog that had been bitten by a viper (p.99) also contributes to the representation of the Natale family as ungenerous and lacking in compassion.

Michele is grateful for Salvatore's intervention, and again expresses his affection for his best friend. Salvatore's invitation to "play Subbuteo" (p.103) introduces the game that comes to symbolise the difference in socio-economic status between the two friends, a difference that threatens to divide them permanently in the following chapter.

Michele and Pino: A father–son talk

Pino tells Michele that they have "got to talk" (p.105), which leads into the first of two conversations between Pino and Michele demonstrating the complexities of their relationship. The strength of the bond between them is evident, especially when Pino holds his son tightly, whispering "Hug me, Michele, hug me!", and Michele cries from the intensity of his feelings (pp.106–7). However, the scene also shows Pino to be evasive and distracted in dealing with his son. Michele knows that his father is refusing to tell him the truth about Sergio since he has observed the authority the old man has over Pino, and knows that Sergio 'was his boss' (p.106). Pino also avoids answering Michele's questions about his work in the North, just as Michele does not fully answer his father's questions about where he rides during the day. The distance between them, exacerbated by their inability to communicate their most pressing thoughts, seems greater than ever at the conclusion of this conversation.

"The world's a place full of holes"

Michele tells Filippo about his mother's appearance on television, but Filippo thinks his entire family is dead and in holes. He also thinks that he can only see in the dark and that the wash-bears talk to him; Filippo has clearly retreated from any engagement with reality into an imaginative existence that minimises his sense of loss. His insistence on covering himself with the blanket is symptomatic of this retreat, although his willingness to let Michele join him under it is the first sign that Filippo is open to Michele's friendship. Indeed, this scene greatly advances the friendship between the boys, as they discover that they are the same age and in the same year at school.

Michele washes Filippo's face, demonstrating not merely his capacity to help, but also how his fear of Filippo's strangeness – previously manifest as an aversion to touching or being touched by Filippo – dissipates as he realises that their similarities far outweigh their differences. The act of cleaning Filippo's encrusted eyes is extremely symbolic, representing Filippo's renewed interaction with the world. His new sense of the future, of *having* a future, is signalled when he makes Michele promise to return – a promise that Michele takes extremely seriously.

Foiling the monsters

Michele's night-time strategy for dealing with his fear of monsters is to imagine them entering a bus, which then morphs into his stomach. This provides another perspective on the theme of entrapment, which to this point has been developed through images of cruelty, such as Italo Natale's dogs confined to their kennels (p.66) or Filippo's being chained in the hole. Michele's imagined procession of monsters into his stomach shows how entrapment is a response to fear – an attempt to displace the entities that cause fear. The way in which individuals try to control the freedoms of others in order to suppress their own fear becomes a central preoccupation of the narrative.

One person of whom Michele clearly has every reason to be afraid is Sergio, yet Michele's first conversation with the old man actually eases his anxieties. Sergio's account of the deterioration of his relationships with his two sons, emphasising that other people are to blame for their problems rather than taking responsibility himself, complements the narrative about Michele's own problems with his father.

Sergio clearly has little sympathy for alternative viewpoints or different cultures, and his black-and-white attitudes – Francesco "was a good boy", "Slavs are the worst" (p.116) – contrast with Michele's intuitive understanding of individual complexities. Nevertheless, Michele is drawn into Sergio's story about Francesco's mysterious death on the spectacular Amalfi coast and the suspicious nature of his wife's role in it.

Sergio does not suggest that his son is also involved in criminal activities or that his murder might have been a revenge killing; these possibilities are part of the unwritten subtext of Sergio's narrative. Also unspecified is exactly what kind of action Sergio took against his daughter-in-law, with his refusal to divulge any more than "I gave her …" effectively conveying Sergio's capacity for violence (p.118).

Q What does the story of Maria's burnt Barbie Doll tell you about Michele's tendency to confuse story and reality?

Q What do the descriptions of Sergio's body – his 'sunken eyes', 'flaccid skin' and so on (p.115) – indicate about his lifestyle?

(Chapter 6) (pp.119–58)

Summary: *Michele tells Salvatore about Filippo in exchange for a Subbuteo team; he takes Filippo out of the hole; Felice discovers Michele in the hole; Salvatore betrays Michele; Felice fights with Teresa, then is overpowered by Pino and Sergio.*

Michele searches through Sergio's suitcase, finding articles corroborating the story about Francesco's death and Filippo's exercise book. He also finds Sergio's gun, which reappears dramatically in the final chapter (p.194). When Michele goes out for breakfast Teresa is singing and dancing while doing the housework, and Michele is able to joke along with her about sharing his room with Sergio. Maria joins in and Teresa carries both her children while dancing around the room. This is a rare moment of familial happiness; significantly, Pino is absent. The promise of going "to the seaside next week" (p.123) shows how both Teresa and Pino cling to an optimistic view of their situation and of their ability to escape from it.

Helping Felice

Michele takes a cake to Salvatore's mother not as a gift but to sell it, reflecting the different social statuses of the two families. On the way, Michele encounters Felice trapped beneath his 127; once again, Michele helps someone in distress, though in this case he is motivated more by fear of the consequences of *not* helping than by his innate sensitivity.

Felice is pleased to be released, but rather than thanking Michele he begins cursing Sergio. He is clearly frustrated by his personal circumstances, but the only way he seems able to deal with them is through violence. When he suspects he has said too much, he threatens Michele with a knife that he clearly is willing to use, anticipating the more serious confrontation between them a few hours later.

The arrogance of the Scardacciones

The Scardacciones' house contrasts in every way with Michele's, but its description does not suggest that it is a more attractive home. Although it is very imposing, possessing a 'marble stairway', 'a big room with angels painted on the ceiling' and a 'medieval suit of armour' (pp.126–7), Michele emphasises its claustrophobic 'musty atmosphere' (p.127). Its 'shutters were never opened' during the day and Michele compares the feeling of being inside it to 'being in a church' (p.127) – that is, for someone so comfortable being outdoors, not a positive feeling at all.

Michele's portrait of Salvatore's mother, Letizia Scardaccione, and her sister Lucilla, stresses their difference from his own mother, who is extremely active and domestically competent. These women, in contrast, sit 'all day long in two armchairs' (p.127) and depend on the maid, Antonia, to do all of the housework. The lack of variety and interest in their lives is reflected in their ridiculous teasing of Michele about marrying eighteen-year-old Antonia. Letizia's condescension towards Michele, when she offers him Salvatore's old clothes and suggests that he looks poorly dressed, suggests that she has a high opinion of her own judgment and social position. However, this opinion seems to be based only on her family's superior wealth and is undermined by her every action and remark.

Michele trades his secret for a soccer team

Michele visits Salvatore in his room, passing Nunzio's room on the way. Nunzio's situation, confined in a mental hospital, is another reminder of how innocent people can be incarcerated; such entrapment is not only the result of criminal actions (such as Filippo's kidnapping) but of the regular operations of society. Salvatore, though, seems to have every luxury and freedom: a large room, a piano and record player, and – most significantly of all from Michele's perspective – a Subbuteo cloth and complete set of teams. In this room, the differences between the two boys seem most apparent and, to Michele, most unjust. Michele is moved to think that his father 'didn't care' about him, and that Salvatore 'was stingy' (p.132). There is some evidence to support both of these opinions, but it is so uncharacteristic of Michele to think in these ways that is easier to read the following events as temporary aberrations.

After keeping his knowledge of Filippo's plight a secret for several days, Michele's desire to possess his own Subbuteo team leads him to trade his secret for a material object – the 'jinxed' players of Lanerossi Vicenza. Of course, there is nothing illegal in this exchange, but on one level Michele participates here in the same kind of morally questionable transaction as the adults do in kidnapping Filippo. Michele wants something that he cannot obtain by conventional means, so he obtains it by more dubious means.

Michele feels he has done the wrong thing almost immediately. Although telling Salvatore everything he has learnt covertly in the previous five days gives him a 'wonderful feeling' (p.134), the comparison he makes with eating an excessive amount of 'peaches in syrup' (p.134) and subsequently being violently ill reflects a degree of self-indulgence in the act. Curiously, Salvatore appears completely uninterested in Filippo's situation or in the adults' cruelty. This reinforces our conception of Salvatore as rather aloof and haughty, already suggested by his inclination to play Subbuteo (a game obviously designed for two players) or with his toy soldiers on his own (p.131). Michele becomes disheartened, regretting that he has traded Filippo's story so thoughtlessly.

Just as the adults lose control of the kidnapping – of the exchange of the boy for money – Michele loses control of his knowledge of Filippo by 'selling' it to Salvatore. Michele compares what he has done with the actions of Judas 'who had bartered Jesus for thirty pieces of silver' (p.135); what Michele has gained is of far less value than what has been sold.

Salvatore's betrayal

Filippo's hole has been cleaned and his foot bandaged and relieved of the chain, indicating for the first time that his captors have some concern for his welfare. Michele coaxes Filippo out of the hole for a short time, although Filippo's reluctance shows how twisted is his understanding of what has happened to him; he simply cannot comprehend it in rational terms. This in turn suggests that his kidnapping and entrapment are profoundly irrational, contravening a natural order. So, Michele's placing Filippo back amongst nature, sitting him under a tree where he can hear the birds and crickets, helps restore Filippo's sense of his place in the world. He is even able to tell Michele his address in Pavia, but the absence of his mother continues to be incomprehensible to him, and he clings to his belief that she must be dead

From this point of relative calmness, Michele's sense of contentment and safety rapidly declines. When Felice discovers Michele in the hole with Filippo he initially seems good humoured, but once he has Michele on the ground he throws him against the house with obviously unnecessary force. This scene shows Felice indulging himself in bullying for its own sake, using his physical strength simply because he can.

It is when Michele sees Salvatore sitting in the front seat, though, that he feels most hurt. Salvatore has informed Felice of Michele's clandestine visits, in exchange for a driving lesson. Michele is heartbroken by the apparent ease with which Salvatore has broken their 'vow of eternal friendship' (p.148), especially when Salvatore must know the seriousness of the consequences for Michele.

"You must go away from here"

Felice takes Michele home, only to find that Teresa is furious with him for beating up Michele. Teresa attacks Felice with a frypan, but Felice begins to win the fight, and there is a sexual edge to his violence when Teresa's breast and bottom become exposed. The situation is only resolved when Pino and Sergio come in, and eventually the three men leave the house. Teresa tells Michele: "When you grow up you must go away from here and never come back" (p.154), but Michele actually feels extraordinarily safe in his parents' bed. At night, with Maria asleep beside him and his head on a pillow that 'smelled of papa', Michele has a strong desire to 'stay in their bed forever', to bring about a situation in which 'Nothing would change' (p.154). Change, however, is now the only certain thing in Michele's world.

Michele and Pino

Pino makes Michele promise that he will never see Filippo again, or even talk about Filippo's existence. He provides no explanation or apology for his behaviour; his distress seems entirely due to the fact that the crime has not proceeded smoothly, while his complaint that "The world's wrong" (p.157) seems a pathetic attempt to justify his own wrongdoing. Michele lies to his father about having told Filippo his name, in order to protect not only Michele from harsher punishment but also Filippo from the very real threat of being shot. The distance between father and son continues to increase.

In answer to Michele's question about why they put Filippo in the hole, Pino responds rhetorically: "Didn't you want to go away from Acqua Traverse?" (p.157). Michele answers that he did, but what he doesn't say is that his much deeper wish is for Filippo to be released; that he would never want his own wishes to come true at the expense of another person's freedom or another family's happiness.

Q What is the significance of the image of the bus trapped in a storm and 'sinking silently', the monsters inside unable to escape (p.155)?

(Chapter 7) (pp.159–67)

Summary: *Michele stays at home; he receives a new bicycle.*

Although Michele wakes to a household 'in disarray' (p.159), there is a sense of calmness due to the sleeping adults and the peacefulness of the dawn. This absence of conflict lasts through the day; Teresa cleans the house and the men go out, as if the tensions of the previous day might also simply be packed away.

Michele reads a comic book, *Tex*, the source of his American Indian idol Tiger Jack, but his thoughts continue to dwell on Filippo's predicament. He is especially concerned that Filippo's trust in him will go unrewarded, since Michele is unable to keep his promise to return. Even now that his and Filippo's physical wellbeing is so seriously threatened, Michele continues to place an extremely high value on ethical behaviour – as if the worst thing that could happen is not to be injured, but to lose somebody's good opinion of you, to be judged untrustworthy. It is an attitude Michele has learned from his parents, but which they themselves seem to have recklessly discarded.

Gifts

Perhaps as an attempt to 'buy' Michele's future obedience, his father gives him a new bicycle, similar to one which Michele saw and coveted in a shop. Michele is disappointed in his 'present', since he initially hoped that his father had brought Filippo to the house. As always, Michele is far more interested in human contact than with acquiring material possessions.

Maria, though, is delighted with her gift of a new Barbie doll. If these children are isolated in a geographical sense, popular, consumer culture (dolls and comic strips) is nevertheless an everyday part of their lives. Maria names her doll Barbara, since Barbara has said she will grow up to be like Barbie. From what we know about Barbara this seems an unlikely eventuality, but these children's aspirations are clearly not bound by the culture that belongs to the particular place of their upbringing.

Sergio's life in Brazil

Michele shares his room for another evening with Sergio, who again seems willing to talk, showing no ill-will towards Michele for the additional anxiety he has caused the adults. However, the more Sergio says, the less attractive a person he appears. He kills a moth casually, raising the possibility that he could kill a person with as little thought for the consequences. His Cadillac, bought second-hand "in perfect condition" (p.167), prompts questions about the means by which he has come by it (did he have its previous owner killed?), and one also wonders about the nature of the relationship between this old, unattractive man and his twenty-three-year-old wife.

Finally, the photo of the huge piece of speck, a cured and smoked form of pork, says less about Sergio's refined taste than about his seemingly insatiable greed; his suggestion that he went to great trouble to bring it to his wife is not particularly credible. Far more believable is Sergio's claim that he likes Brazil because things are cheap and "Everybody serving you" (p.167), showing how lazy and arrogant he really is.

(Chapter 8) (pp.168–73)

Summary: *Michele resists returning to the abandoned house; Michele and Salvatore reconcile.*

After such a dramatic week, in which each of the seven days brings a crucial new piece of information or moment of conflict, nothing happens for some time. Although Michele desperately wants to return to Filippo – as he had promised – he refrains from doing so. Nevertheless, his rides on his new bicycle, the Red Dragon, lead ever closer to the abandoned house, reflecting the strength of the bond between Michele and Filippo. Michele imagines that the surrounding hills are animated by an inner life, inhabited by fantastical creatures that 'rise up like waves of the ocean' (p.170). Michele imagines these sinister, primeval forces threatening Filippo; even at this point he cannot quite believe in the evil of men.

Michele and Salvatore make peace

Unexpectedly, a moment of redemption takes place. While playing 'Den free everybody' at the carob, Salvatore joins forces with Michele in order to defeat Skull; in fact, Salvatore offers to lose so that Michele can win. This act of generosity wins instant acceptance from Michele, who shakes Salvatore's hand with pleasure. Salvatore looks forward to the next school year, while Michele talks about leaving Acqua Traverse and going "To the North" (p.172). For Michele, the North retains its magical appeal, its possibilities of pleasure and freedom. Salvatore, though, is more content with the possibilities of the here-and-now.

The game concludes on a positive note for Michele and Salvatore, since their combined effort results in them both reaching the carob and defeating Skull. Their final cry, "Den free everybody!" (p.173), has clear resonances for the text's overall message: all innocent people should be free from capture and entrapment. Just how to liberate those who are imprisoned, however, is a problem that Michele now needs to confront not simply in a game, but in real life.

(Chapter 9) (pp.174–87)

Summary: *The children return to the abandoned farmhouse; Filippo is no longer in the hole; police helicopters appear overhead.*

The storm approaches

The storm clouds gathering on the horizon indicate that the long summer drought is coming to an end; they also suggest, metaphorically, that the tensions of the summer are soon to be resolved, perhaps violently. The clouds that 'started to advance on Acqua Traverse' (p.174) anticipate the advance on the isolated village of the forces of law and order, embodied by the two *Carabinieri* helicopters that appear near the end of the chapter.

Wasps making their nest

As Michele lies in the shed with the other children he observes some wasps making a nest, persisting with their task despite Remo's repeated destruction of the nest. The image of the wasps is a very significant one, suggesting that strong natural forces underpin family bonds and reminding us of Michele's love of the natural world. Both of these concepts feature again in the final chapter, when the circling of the owl above the gully provides the crucial clue to Filippo's location. Moreover, Michele's recollection that his father told him about the wasps building their nest because "It's in their nature" (p.175) shows how Pino remains for Michele the arbiter of knowledge; Michele still does not question his father's wisdom, even after everything he has learnt.

The return to the hole

Skull suggests returning to the abandoned house, and Michele reluctantly agrees. He is desperate to fulfil his promise to Filippo, yet simultaneously terrified of the consequences of breaking the oath he has made to his father. The encroaching thunderstorm reflects Michele's increasing emotional tension; the outside world mirrors the inner, psychological one. The storm breaks as they arrive at the house, which makes Michele think of Filippo being drowned in the hole.

However, Filippo's hole is empty, which initially makes Michele despair for the loss of his friend: 'he was mine and … they had taken him away from me' (p.183). Salvatore, who has overheard his father talking to Pino and Sergio, tells Michele that Filippo has been hidden in the gravina at Melichetti's, thus revealing that the kidnapping plot remains unfinished. Michele reflects once again on his father's advice that "Monsters don't exist. It's men you should be afraid of" (p.184). At this point he thinks of another instance of animal behaviour, one that is akin to the cruel behaviour of men, or of children such as Remo and Skull who care nothing about the suffering of other creatures.

Like cats playing with lizards

The image of cats playing with lizards, torturing them throughout a protracted death as if to 'amuse' themselves (p.184), is important since it complicates the otherwise largely sentimental view of nature presented by the narrative. Michele notes the similarity between the cruel behaviour of the adults, in particular his father, and the behaviour of cats that use their hunting prowess not for survival but for more frivolous acts. It is this behaviour that Michele identifies as belonging to 'monsters'.

If this image reinforces Filippo's vulnerability in the hands of ruthless and greedy men, the tension is raised still further when two police helicopters fly over the children's heads. Back at the village, the adults have responded to the appearance of the *Carabinieri* by gathering in the Scardacciones' house, leaving the children to fend for themselves for the evening. The chapter closes with Michele and Maria walking hand in hand back to their house, in the novel's most poignant image of the fragmentation of family life.

Q How does the image of bales of hay 'like pawns on a chessboard' (p.177) also relate to the narrative events and characters at this point?

Q What is the significance of Michele's realisation that the Red Dragon is 'a rip-off' (p.178)?

(Chapter 10) (pp.188–215)

Summary: *Sergio points a gun at Felice; the men play 'the soldier's draw' to determine who will shoot Filippo; Michele rides to Melichetti's; Filippo escapes, but Michele is shot by his own father.*

Sergio, Pietro Mura, Felice, Pino and Teresa gather once again in the Amitranos' kitchen, as the tension mounts over what is to be done with Filippo. Michele perceives that they are attempting to conceal their fear with hostility towards each other, and once again he draws on his understanding of the natural world to provide an image, or analogy, by which to explain their behaviour. He compares the adults to 'green lizards' which 'swell up and spit and try to scare you because they're more scared of you' (p.189), reducing their display of power and strength to mere posturing and performance.

Teresa tries to cope

Teresa brings Michele and Maria some food, but she breaks down, unable to suppress the effects of such sustained tension. All three begin to cry, but Teresa refuses to talk openly to her children, taking refuge in silence as a means of denying her true situation. In order to force Michele and Maria also to be silent, she pushes their pillows over their heads; the children pretend to sleep not because they are genuinely calmed, but to placate their mother. Although Teresa asserts her authority here, this scene actually shows her at her most vulnerable, completely unable to cope with the traumatic situation the family, and indeed the entire village, is now in.

The men resort to violence

After Teresa leaves the room, Michele opens the door just enough to follow the dramatic events in the kitchen, where the adults debate their, and Filippo's, futures. Sergio has accused Felice of being homosexual, showing how the accusations between the men now have nothing to do with how they have handled the kidnapping but are simply at the level of personal insults. Sergio contemptuously dismisses Pino's humane suggestion that they return Filippo to his mother. After this point, the only course of action that seems possible to the men is one of violence.

Felice strikes the old man, who is so badly hurt that even Michele feels sorry for him. Sergio, though, is as defiant as ever, and taunts Felice with his earlier declarations of courage and strength:

> You said you'd do it and you chickened out. What was it you said? Slit him open like a lamb, I will, no problem, I'm not scared. (p.193)

Key point

The appearance of the novel's title here marks this as a key speech, one that points to the always ironic nature of the claim 'I'm not scared'; a claim that is only ever made when fear is precisely the emotion being experienced.

In response to Felice's continued attempts to harm him, Sergio points his gun against the young man's forehead, making further bloodshed seem inevitable. Pino resolves the situation by proposing they play the game introduced into the narrative in its opening chapter, 'the soldier's draw', to decide which of the men will shoot Filippo (p.195). Michele has no interest in whose fate this will be; his only concern is to save Filippo, whereas the only concern of the adults is to preserve themselves.

Michele rides to Melichetti's

Michele's desperate ride to Melichetti's forces him to confront all of his worst fears: the darkness; the prospect of giants; Melichetti's pigs; and the imminent arrival of the adults, bent on using violence to solve their problems. He negotiates these fears through the force of his imagination, pretending to be the character Tiger Jack from the *Tex* comic strip. Thus, Michele deals with his fear of the pigs, which may or may not be well-founded – after all, it is based only on stories told by Skull – by smearing himself with 'piss-soaked earth' (p.203). In a way, he becomes like the thing he fears, rather than opposing himself to it and trying to exterminate it.

In the gravina, Michele faces another obstacle: he has no way of determining Filippo's location. At this point, the narrative makes one final use of Michele's close knowledge of natural phenomena, through the figure of the owl circling insistently above a pile of stakes on the ground. The owl's presence is a sign that her nest has been covered over, and thus a sign of Filippo's makeshift prison.

Filippo is bound, gagged and ill, too fatigued to try to escape. Michele too is so tired that he falls asleep, reflecting the toll that his physical and emotional investment in saving Filippo has taken on him. Their shared experience of adversity has drawn the two boys close together, naked, cold and exhausted. Michele's early feelings of repulsion at physical contact with Filippo are now replaced by a tender intimacy: 'I embraced him' (p.211), then later 'I put my arms around him as if he was a rag doll' (p.212).

When a barking dog and men's voices wake him, Michele knows that this is the last possible moment to act. He convinces Filippo to climb out of the hole and hide, with the physical contact between the boys again showing how their survival depends on their mutual trust and affection. Indeed, Filippo is physically dependent on Michele to make his escape. Equally important, though, is Michele's assurance that "There's nothing to be scared of" (p.214), to counter Filippo's "I'm scared" (p.214). Of course, Michele knows – as does the reader – that there is every reason to be scared. Nevertheless, the positive message of these few words counteracts the weight of reality, and achieves the desired effect: Filippo attains his freedom.

In a twist that in many ways is anticipated by the narrative throughout, but that nevertheless effects a stunning climax for the novel, Michele is shot by his father when he is unable to escape from the hole. When he regains consciousness, Michele is in his father's arms, covered in blood and in terrible pain. Dogs and men, and a helicopter, are nearby. Michele knows they are not monsters, but they are as terrifying, as irresistibly powerful, as monsters, and even at this point he wishes his father to flee. Pino, though, at last seems willing to face the world honestly; he is crying, a pathetic and isolated figure, but as he pleads for help and understanding he regains a degree of humility. However there is no response, and the narrative concludes enigmatically, without indicating whether the approaching dark, silent figure represents a threat of further violence or a promise of safety.

Q As Michele jumps from his window he falls 'open-armed' onto the tarpaulin of his father's truck (p.196). What other images like this are there in the narrative (including the epigraph)?

CHARACTERS & RELATIONSHIPS

Michele Amitrano

Key quotes

'I'm Tiger, even better, I'm Tiger's Italian son, I said to myself' (p.44).

'I must pluck up courage and look' (p.60).

'Why didn't they give him back to her? What use was a barmy little boy to them? Filippo's mother was distressed, you could see that' (p.87).

'It was the first time Maria had ever asked me to tell her a bedtime story, I felt very honoured' (p.89).

'I was stretched out on the sacks of wheat, with my head in my hands, quite relaxed, watching the wasps build a nest' (p.174).

Since Michele is the novel's narrator, the society he lives in and the people around him are apprehended through his consciousness. They are coloured by his own assessments of things; by his appreciation of the natural world and his lively imagination; and also by his lack of knowledge of the adult world – his lack of worldliness. Most importantly, Michele's imagination, sensitivity and courage give the narrative its secure moral reference point and its unflinching representation of adult foibles and desires.

Michele's compassion

Michele displays a compassion for the weak and vulnerable almost entirely lacking in those around him. These qualities are immediately established by Michele's stopping to help his sister during the race to the top of the hill – despite his fear of being last. Shortly after, Michele saves Barbara from the embarrassment of having to undress in front of her friends by offering to do the forfeit.

Mostly, though, Michele's sensitivity and compassion are manifest in the way he befriends and eventually attempts to rescue Filippo, despite the ever-increasing danger these actions represent to himself. He hides portions of food in order to have something to take to Filippo; he overcomes his initial feelings of revulsion to clean Filippo's face (p.112); he pushes his own pain to one side in order to push Filippo out of the hole towards freedom (p.212).

Sensitivity to the natural world

Michele has a sense of wonder; this is, of course, a conventional attribute of childhood, but this quality is so much more evident in Michele than in the other children that it is clearly a distinctive aspect of his own personality. In particular, Michele appreciates and finds abundant beauty in the natural world. Even when removing the ticks from Togo's ears he observes the 'little black legs and their dark-brown stomachs' (p.97) of the parasites. Whereas Remo ruthlessly tries to destroy the wasps' nest, Michele wonders: 'Why did those wasps make the nest?' (p.175). This image is particularly poignant because the determination of the wasps to make a home is contrasted with the actions of the village adults that place their own children's wellbeing at great risk.

Imagination and story

Michele's active imagination strongly informs his perceptions of the world. Although at one point he baulks at telling Maria a bedtime story, he actually creates narratives irresistibly, with fantasy and reality continually feeding into each other. Of course, many of Michele's imagined scenarios take the form of horror narratives, featuring fantasy characters such as ogres and witches, or zombie-like beings that rise from death. When he tries to imagine the nature of the connection between the boy in the hole and his own family, Michele makes up a bizarre story about his crazy twin brother who had bitten his mother's nipple and 'tried to tear it off' (p.67). Even Michele's technique of quelling his fears by imagining all the monsters entering a bus (pp.114–15) takes the form of a narrative: not simply a single image, but a series of events, linked (however creatively) by cause and effect, leading to a desired outcome.

Michele inhabits the *Tex* comic-book stories about Tiger Jack so intensely that he pretends he *is* Tiger Jack; this form of role-playing is ultimately empowering, since it helps Michele overcome his fear, especially on the final night. Fascinatingly, as Michele cycles towards Melichetti's farm in the middle of the night he feels that he is 'immersed in ink' (p.197), as if acknowledging that he is both a character in a novel and that his own storytelling capacities are what propel him towards an unknown conclusion.

Pino Amitrano

Key quote

'Papa was the bogeyman. By day he was good, but at night he was bad' (p.87).

"The world's wrong, Michele" (p.157).

Since the first-person narration is from Michele's point of view, little of what motivates his father, Pino, (and to a lesser extent his mother, Teresa) to become involved in Filippo's kidnapping is revealed to the reader. Pino is clearly frustrated by the restricted scope of their lives in Acqua Traverse and his limited means to change their circumstances. When Michele asks him why they have put Filippo in the hole, Pino responds with another question: "Didn't you want to go away from Acqua Traverse?", thus linking the kidnapping with his desire for a better life (p.157).

Pino's despair at the desperate situation they now find themselves in is clearly visible, as he says in a broken voice that "The world's wrong, Michele" (p.157). However, this does not engender much sympathy for Pino, since his own actions are part of what *is* wrong in the novel's world. More significant in retaining the reader's sympathy is Pino's plea on the final night: "let's give him back to her" (p.192). Also, Pino restores a kind of dignity to the group's operations by suggesting the game of 'the soldier's draw' to determine who should shoot Filippo. Unlike Sergio, Pino does not resort to bullying the others to avoid carrying out this most onerous 'duty'.

Teresa Amitrano

Key quote

'She served us and ate standing up' (p.54).

'Mama was dancing and meanwhile she was ironing and singing along' (p.121).

Michele's affection for his mother is unwavering, and unlike his love for Pino, his warm regard for Teresa is reinforced by everything we learn about her. She works continuously and uncomplainingly for her family, 'always on her feet' (p.54); she is 'still beautiful' at the age of thirty-three, yet in no way vain, and men's 'lecherous looks just slipped off her' (p.54).

Teresa's desire to protect Michele from harm is clear when she unhesitatingly attacks Felice (p.151), but on the whole she is much more inclined than Pino to express her affection for her children in a playful manner, such as when she sings and dances with them one morning (pp.121–3). However, there is a strange moment when Teresa, 'getting desperate', places pillows on the heads of Michele and Maria in order to stop them talking and to stop them hearing the men arguing in the next room (p.190).

Teresa becomes overwhelmed by her family's precarious situation, but she never questions her husband's judgment or role in the kidnapping. This makes her character more complicated than Michele's idealistic portrayal of her allows, and it remains unclear just how far Teresa is implicated in the kidnapping plot. On the very first night Michele sees his parents' feet 'intertwined' in bed (p.40), and they remain supportive of each other throughout the crisis.

That Teresa never questions Sergio's presence in the house or argues for a more compassionate treatment of Filippo perhaps reflects not so much her approval of the plot, but rather the strongly patriarchal nature of the society, in which women have virtually no power or independence.

Salvatore Scardaccione

Key quotes

'He was a loner' (p.3).

'I liked Salvatore. I liked the way he always kept calm and didn't fly off the handle every five minutes' (p.103).

'Salvatore was stingy' (p.132).

Salvatore is Michele's best friend, but his most significant action in the novel is to betray Michele. His family is the wealthiest in the (otherwise poor) village, but perhaps a stronger influence on his character is the way his parents do not seem to interact with him. His father, the Avvocato Emilio Scardaccione, is often away in Rome, and his mother sits with her sister 'all day long in two armchairs which they had worn out' (p.127). Salvatore's home life lacks the warmth and closeness of Michele's, suggesting that the fact that he 'often kept to himself' (p.3) owes much to his upbringing – reinforcing the importance placed by the novel on a nurturing home environment.

That Michele even feels compelled to exchange his secret for Salvatore's Lanerossi team reflects badly on Salvatore. The gulf between the boys' social and material status is most evident in this scene, when Michele visits Salvatore and begs for a Subbuteo team of his own. Salvatore takes for granted the privileges of wealth – a Subbuteo set with twelve full teams, piano lessons, a large room all to himself – that Michele can never even hope to possess. All Michele asks for is one team, and Salvatore's refusal reflects the selfishness of an overindulged child, with no inclination to part with things that are surplus to his own needs. Nor does Salvatore show any compassion for Filippo, further suggesting that his comfortable standard of living has somehow made him feel superior to others less fortunate.

Nevertheless, Salvatore's positive attributes are also apparent early in the narrative. For this reason, Salvatore is an important character in Ammaniti's overall attempt to represent people as inherently complex, as sometimes flawed in their responses to circumstances but almost never absolutely good or evil. Michele admires the way in which Salvatore is not completely under the sway of Skull's dominance of the group of children, and also the way in which Salvatore 'always kept calm' (p.103). Salvatore's taciturn disposition may lead to him being 'a loner' (p.3), but it also enables him to defuse tense situations, a quality sorely lacking amongst the adults of the village. He is a valuable foil to Michele, who is extremely impressionable and impulsive.

Salvatore's attempt to make up for his betrayal is successful, showing that he is not simply a selfish child of rich parents. It also suggests that he has come to realise how significant the loss of Michele's friendship is. His later admission to Michele that he knows where Filippo's new hiding place is confirms Salvatore's changed attitude, from wanting to keep things to himself to being willing to impart something (knowledge) valued by another.

Filippo Carducci

Key quotes

"They're all dead and they live in holes like this one ... The world's a place full of holes with dead people in them" (pp.109–10).

"I knew you would. You promised" (p.136).

Filippo is the son of Giovanni and Luisa Carducci, and his kidnapping and incarceration are at the centre of the novel's action. That the actions of the kidnappers are morally (not to mention legally) aberrant is reinforced by Filippo's quirky and increasingly endearing personality; if Filippo was as unsympathetic a character as some of the children of Acqua Traverse, the adults' crime would not seem nearly as evil. His affection for the 'little wash-bears' and for his family's ancient gardener, Peppino, are evident in the passage Michele reads in Filippo's exercise book (pp.120–1). Like Michele, Filippo's instincts are to appreciate and protect the weak, the vulnerable and the innocent.

Filippo is from a very well-off family, reflected in the fact that he has an electric train set (p.86) and that his mother appears 'in a big leather armchair in a room full of books' (p.86). His values, though, seem identical to those of Michele: loyalty, honesty and the pleasure of companionship are prized above any material possession. Filippo trusts Michele's promise to return absolutely, a level of trust Michele finds hard to come by in others.

Filippo's strange ideas

If Filippo's ideas seem eccentric to Michele, they might largely be explained by the radical way in which Filippo's world has been turned upside down. From being always clean and well dressed he has become perpetually dirty and naked; from having close contact with his mother he is deprived, except during Michele's brief visits, of company and affection. It is not very surprising, then, that he believes the entire world has been inverted: that he, and all those close to him, have died; that the world's "full of holes with dead people in them" (p.110); that Michele is an angel (p.140). Like Michele, Filippo uses the few facts at his disposal to generate stories that, however loosely tethered they are to reality, help him to make sense of his situation.

Barbara Mura

Of the children of Acqua Traverse, eleven-year-old Barbara is at the bottom of the social hierarchy, the one who 'always gets all the bad luck' (p.18). She is unfairly victimised by Skull, who exploits her vulnerability to satisfy his own nascent curiosity about girls. Even when she is bullied and slapped across the face by Skull, she clings to the remnants of her dignity, 'suppressing her sobs' and pointing out to the other children their complicity in Skull's cruelty (p.20).

Michele does not encourage the reader to be entirely sympathetic to Barbara, accusing her of being duplicitous 'as soon as she got the chance' (p.10) and emphasising how fat and ugly she seems to him.

So Barbara's charms emerge 'between the lines', from what Michele describes of her actions rather than how he says he feels about her. Her attempt to relieve Togo of his ticks seems misguided but well-intentioned, despite Michele's suspicions that she intends to kill the poor dog. She does, after all, promise Togo that she will take him to Lucignano for an ice-cream (p.96), and she is the only one of the children to provide Togo with regular attention. Togo, in return, knows that Barbara is an unfailing source of comfort, fleeing to her lap when Skull tries to kick him (p.102).

Touched by Michele's rescuing her from the forfeit and his help with Togo's tick infestation, Barbara asks him to be her boyfriend. His rejection is another confirmation of her outsider status amongst the children, but she receives it with aplomb and walks off with her self-respect intact (pp.98–9). Interestingly, after this Michele does not make any more disparaging comments about Barbara.

The Natale family: Felice, Antonio and Italo

The men of the Natale family represent much that is bad in the human character, which is ironic since 'Natale' is the Italian word for 'Christmas'. They seem unable to feel sympathy or show compassion for another person, or even to an animal. Italo keeps his dogs locked up 'behind wire netting' (p.66), and on one occasion refuses to take to a vet a dog that has been bitten by a viper (p.99). Italo is more concerned by the possibility that going to the vet will be a "Waste of money" (p.99) than with alleviating the animal's suffering.

This indifference to suffering is also reflected in the Natales' relations with other people. Antonio Natale is known as Skull, as if he is dead to human feeling; as the unchallenged leader of the village children he takes every opportunity to humiliate them, especially Barbara. In any situation, Skull thinks only of how he might benefit. He even makes the most of Michele's new bike, showing off his ability to ride through the village 'on one wheel' (p.168). When he doesn't get his own way the threat of violence is never far away, so that Michele is always wary of the possibility that 'Skull could suddenly flip and decide to pull you off your bike and beat you up' (p.103).

Felice Natale – whose name, incongruously, means 'Happy Christmas' – is an even more terrifying figure: 'a thousand times worse' (p.69). Although Michele is clearly justified in being afraid of Felice, some fascinating complexities to Felice's character emerge. The scene in which Felice sings along with the radio, performing both male and female roles to Michele's considerable enjoyment, shows something of a personality that can simply find no expression within the narrow life of the village. At twenty years of age he has no friends in the area, and as Michele acknowledges: 'Felice in Acqua Traverse was like a tiger in a cage' (p.70). He is certainly capable of violence, but his violent tendency comes to the fore when he is most afraid. He strikes Sergio, for instance, partly in retaliation for being called a 'poof', but partly out of fear of being made to kill Filippo; he pleads not to have to do this: "Why should *I* have to do it, why?" (p.194).

Michele describes the contradictory nature of Felice's appearance, the thuggish look he cultivates through wearing 'combat jackets and camouflaged trousers' contrasting with his 'little gappy teeth like a baby crocodile's' (p.70). Felice has a man's body and is given adult responsibilities, but psychologically he continues to have a child's simplistic approach to emotional tensions. Like his younger brother, Felice seeks to resolve conflict by violent means, and is completely stymied when such an approach does achieve the desired outcome.

Sergio Materia

A seventy-seven-year-old man who is a hardened criminal, Sergio is the leader of the kidnappers: 'like the emperor' is Michele's simile for Sergio's authority amongst the village adults. However, unlike an enlightened ruler, Sergio's descriptions of his life show that he has almost no consideration for anybody other than himself. His affection for Brazil – a place that Sergio characterises in terms of: "Everybody serving you. You don't do shit all day" (p.167) – reflects only his own laziness and greed. On the other hand, his self-confidence and charisma, despite his ageing and deteriorating body, almost make Michele feel comfortable in his presence. Michele is curious enough to ask Sergio questions about his life, which appears exotic and dangerous from a young, provincial Italian boy's perspective.

The casualness with which Sergio squashes a moth and curses "Fucking moths" (p.166) suggests he could kill a person just as efficiently. The reader is left wondering what precisely is the nature of the punishment Sergio meted out to his daughter-in-law following the death of his son, Francesco: "that bitch paid for it" is all we learn (p.118). Indeed, it is almost a surprise that Sergio does not pull the trigger when he places his gun against Felice's forehead (p.194). Sergio's character is all the more menacing for the fact that his capacity for violence is barely restrained, hinted at rather than explicitly demonstrated.

Sergio's authority is immediately apparent to Michele when he observes the impunity with which Sergio accuses and insults the other adults, including Michele's father. However, there is another aspect to Sergio that Michele draws our attention to, the frailty of his old and ill-treated body. His many hours of drinking and smoking have left his 'sunken eyes ... tinged with red' (p.115) and Michele repeatedly notes how thin and emaciated the old man's body is, especially his legs: "I kept looking at those thin, white, hairless calves' (p.193). The complete absence of muscles suggests a life of indolence, in which any kind of physical exertion is performed by others. In a way, Sergio is a living example of a creature from one of Michele's nightmares, a dead man who is walking around on earth: one who is morally and spiritually bankrupt, whose body is so lacking in life that only skin and bones remain.

Fathers and sons

Key quote

'I hugged him as hard as I could and I couldn't help crying' (p.107).

"My boys didn't like me either" (Sergio, p.116).

The relationship between Pino and Michele is perhaps the central relationship in the narrative because so much of what Michele thinks and does is informed by it: he fears his father's anger; he desires his father's approval; he has, at least initially, absolute trust in his father's judgment and wisdom. In many ways the story of the novel is the story of the evolving relationship between Michele and Pino. This relationship is set against a series of stories and examples of other father-son relationships throughout the text.

Other fathers and sons

Stories about problems in father-son relationships include one about a werewolf, who is actually the town pharmacist, shot by a hunter who turns out to be the werewolf's son (p.48); and Salvatore's story about the father who asks a wizard to bring his dead son back to life. The resurrected son is so grotesque that the father is forced to set fire to him. Both stories pre-empt, through their violent ends, the last moments of the novel, in which Pino inadvertently shoots his own son.

Other father-son relationships in the novel are also fraught. Sergio tells Michele about his two sons, one of whom he thinks "might as well be dead" while the other has died mysteriously after having been "taken for a ride" by his wife (pp.116–17). The Avvocato Emilio Scardaccione is almost never home to be a father to Salvatore, which seems to contribute to Salvatore's tendency to be 'a loner' (p.3). These fathers are distant yet imposing figures to their sons; Pino, in contrast, has a natural ease in relating to Michele, which makes the deterioration of their relationship all the more moving.

Different personal journeys

Until the last moment of the novel, Pino is never violent towards Michele, but he displays no real interest in or understanding of his son's emotional life. The two seem to drift apart as they feel constrained from communicating freely with each other, and as they follow quite different, and ultimately opposed, moral pathways. On the very first evening, Pino arm-wrestles Michele, clearly wanting him to become a conventional, strong male figure. Yet what Michele has – loyalty, kindness, imagination – are far more valuable qualities than physical strength, and it is one of the tragedies of the novel that Pino does not appreciate his son's real strengths.

The Crock

Michele's devotion to his father is unwavering, even surviving the new knowledge Michele gains about what Pino has done and is capable of. The clearest symbol of this devotion is Michele's bicycle, known as 'the Crock', which Michele introduces almost as a character in the story by stating: 'I liked it, it was my father's' (p.6). Michele's pride in having his father's old bike is reaffirmed in his story about seeing a new bike in Lucignano, when he had justified his possession of the Crock to the shop assistant by saying "It used to be papa's" (p.163). For his desperate last ride of the novel, Michele prefers the 'old Crock' to the new 'Red Dragon', reflecting the persistence of his belief not just in the bike, but in the indestructible nature of the bond he has with his father.

Friendships

Key quotes

'I liked Salvatore. I liked the way he always kept calm and didn't fly off the handle every five minutes' (p.103).

"He's a friend of mine" (Pino to Michele, about Sergio, p.106).

'He was my best friend. Once, on a branch of the carob, we had even made a vow of eternal friendship' (p.148).

'I embraced him' (p.211).

Michele has two close friends: Salvatore and Filippo. The first friendship is long-established; Michele introduces Salvatore as his 'best friend' (p.3), and later recalls that they had 'even made a vow of eternal friendship' (p.148). However, even this friendship is fragile, and Salvatore's betrayal almost destroys it. Just as the events of the novel show how familial relationships are vulnerable to individual aspirations, Salvatore's betrayal also suggests that in friendships there are no guarantees.

In this light, Salvatore's offer to help Michele win the game of 'Den free everybody', which both boys know is also a request for forgiveness, is an extraordinarily positive moment. Michele grasps the opportunity for the restoration of their friendship at once, indicating that its continuity requires a mutual commitment but, given that, even seemingly irreparable ruptures between friends can be healed. In this way, the text suggests that friendships may be fragile, but they are also resilient. The benefits of such a cooperative spirit are immediately demonstrated, with both boys (rather than just one) reaching the carob to defeat Skull.

Michele and Filippo

The second of Michele's friendships develops rapidly over the course of a few days, as his pity and fascination for Filippo's degraded condition turn into a genuine pleasure in Filippo's company. The two boys are from very different social classes, reflected in the fact that Michele is from Italy's south while Filippo is from the more prosperous north, but this difference is immaterial to their interaction. They are the same age, but more tellingly they share a rich imaginative life. Just as Michele's mind is full of witches, ogres and other kinds of monsters, Filippo imagines that he has died, and that the 'little wash-bears' are talking to him, occasionally even telling lies (p.74).

While Salvatore seems to be contented with his own company, Filippo comes to depend on Michele for human contact and affection. Michele, too, finds increasing intimacy in his friendship with Filippo, embracing him when they are both 'shivering with cold' on the final night before holding and pushing him up out of the hole (pp.211–13).

Although Filippo does not actually die and then come back to life, Michele's friendship does have this kind of effect on Filippo; he gradually coaxes from Filippo a few words of conversation, then an appetite, and finally, and most decisively, a desire to achieve freedom.

Friendship versus power

These friendships involving Michele contrast markedly with others in the text. Pino claims that Sergio is a friend (pp.63, 106), but the two men never show each other any courtesy, let alone affection. Their relationship seems purely one of convenience, for the purposes of carrying out a crime. Amongst the children, Skull and Remo appear to be friends, but Remo is entirely subservient to Skull, obediently performing whatever activity the older boy demands. These friendships are not lacking in loyalty, but they are founded on power, not on mutual respect.

THEMES, IDEAS & VALUES

Fear and moral obligations

Key quotes

'"I'm not scared of anything," I whispered to hearten myself, but my legs were wobbly and a voice in my brain was screaming at me not to go' (p.46).

'But I was scared. What if I found papa and the old man at the house?' (p.95).

'Green lizards, when they can't get away and you're about to catch them, open their mouths, swell up and spit and try to scare you because they're more scared of you ... ' (p.189).

"What was it you said? Slit him open like a lamb, I will, no problem, I'm not scared" (Sergio to Felice, p.193).

"You're not scared. There's nothing to be scared of" (Michele to Filippo, p.214).

As the title signals, the way in which we experience fear and allow fear to influence, or even stymie, our actions is at the centre of this novel's thematic preoccupations. The title is a denial of fear – that is, an assertion of courage and boldness – that in fact is ironic, since it is contradicted by the experiences of the characters, and especially of the protagonist, Michele. Michele tells himself "I'm not scared of anything" (p.46) when, in fact, he is scared of many things, a number of which are imaginary: ogres, monsters, witches and so on. At first his fear at the abandoned house circulates around these superstitious notions, such as the possibility of dead people coming back to life, but later, when he learns why Filippo is in the hole and who has put him there, Michele's fear gains a more rational basis.

However, even when Michele knows he is right to be afraid, he is compelled to act by his sense of moral obligation. He knows he 'must go' to see Filippo after he hears Filippo's mother's declaration of love on the television, even though he 'was scared' (p.95). Also, after Michele has promised his father not to visit Filippo, he is torn by the fact that he has also promised Filippo that he *will* visit him. It is this latter promise that has the most force, since Michele knows that he 'wouldn't be doing anything wrong' (p.161) and that, without him, Filippo has no-one to provide company or kindness. This sense of obligation – to keep one's word, to be compassionate – is stronger than Michele's fear of what his father might say or do, and the text as a whole endorses Michele's judgment.

Although it is Michele's fear with which the reader becomes most familiar, other characters also experience fear, although they express it, and attempt to conceal it, in different ways. When Michele hears the adults arguing on the final night, he is reminded of green lizards that 'swell up and spit and try to scare you because they're more scared of you' (p.189). Even Felice, who seems to be fearless, shows his fear when confronted with his boast "I'm not scared. I'm a paratrooper" (p.193). He is afraid of being made to kill Filippo, which perhaps is a fear of the consequences, of "doing time" (p.194).

Fear of entrapment

Perhaps the most basic of the novel's moral statements is that entrapment is wrong, but freedom and liberty are inherently good. There are many images of confinement throughout the novel, and each one reinforces the fact that to confine a living creature against its will is a perversion of the natural order (see 'Language: images of cruelty and capture' on page 5 of this text guide). The most heroic action of the novel is Michele's liberation of Filippo, when he urges Filippo to overcome his fear and seek refuge with the words: "You're not scared. There's nothing to be scared of" (p.214).

The fragility of trust

Key quotes

'Salvatore had betrayed me' (p.148).

"I knew you would. You promised" (Filippo to Michele, p.136).

'[H]e would think I didn't want to see him again and I didn't keep my promises. But that wasn't true' (p.162).

Although Michele trusts his friends and family unquestioningly, the ways in which they betray him show how fragile trust is. Trust has to be remade, and it is one of Michele's most endearing qualities that he is always receptive when those close to him try to regain his trust, or show trust in him. Michele is touched by Filippo's trust that he would keep his promise and return (p.136), but once Michele is discovered at the hole this promise becomes very difficult to keep.

As much as Michele worries about Filippo's wellbeing, he also worries that Filippo will think 'I didn't keep my promises' (p.162). Although this might seem relatively unimportant compared to the threat to Filippo's life represented by the adults, the novel thus suggests that when our basic ethical framework is destroyed, the tendency for violence to become the means of settling disputes is almost irresistible.

Even the most seemingly secure relationships are vulnerable in this novel. Salvatore is taken into Michele's trust with regard to the 'secret' about Filippo, but Salvatore betrays this trust, and almost destroys their friendship. Later, when they take part in a game, Salvatore tries to re-establish the friendship by suggesting a means by which Michele can win the game. The strategy depends on Michele trusting Salvatore to do as he says he will – acting as a decoy, distracting Skull so Michele will 'make den' (p.172). Not only does the strategy work, but both boys reach the carob, a sign of their renewed trust and of the possibilities it generates for both of them.

More complex is the trust that Michele places in his father. Even though Michele discovers his father's integral role in Filippo's kidnapping, and witnesses his father threaten to cut off Filippo's ears, he continues to believe what his father says and to trust in his father's essential goodness.

Family bonds

Key quotes

'Why did those wasps make the nest? Who had taught them to do it?' (p.175).

'Swallows, too, if you knock down their nest, keep wheeling round and round till they die of exhaustion' (pp.207–8).

The betrayal of family

The importance of family bonds both to individual happiness and the wellbeing of the community is represented in three main ways. First, there is the devastating effect of the kidnapping on the village; from Michele's point of view, to take Filippo away from his mother is morally wrong, a betrayal of the adults' own family responsibilities. Once Michele thinks of his father as the bogeyman who 'takes the children away and sells them to the gypsies' (p.87), his relationship with his father can never be the same. The deterioration in the bond between them, which stems from Pino's involvement in Filippo's kidnapping, comes to its logical conclusion when Pino attempts to shoot Filippo but instead fires on his own son.

Acquiring values

The second way in which the text represents the importance of family to the wellbeing of the community is through the way in which the children acquire personality traits and moral values from their parents, although the children are also shown to be able to form independent judgments as they acquire experience. In Michele's case, his strong sense of what constitutes right behaviour clearly derives in large part from his upbringing. Both Teresa and Pino are very proud, and continually strive to maintain respectable appearances despite their poverty. When Michele is offered Salvatore's old clothes, he knows that he must refuse because his mother 'said we didn't accept charity from anyone' (p.129).

Pino and Teresa's decision to resort to criminal activity rather than accept charity shows how their strong moral code has been compromised by a desperation to escape from Acqua Traverse. In a sense, their concern with appearances, with the material and financial aspects of life, has outweighed their attachment to the ethical values that underpin society and that they have so successfully instilled in Michele.

The other families also show how children are powerfully influenced by the values of their parents. As the above discussion of the Natale family shows, personal qualities and ways of interacting with others are readily passed from parents to children – especially, in the case of the Natales, from father to sons – simply by the children following their parents' examples. Similarly, when Salvatore betrays Michele, this is seen as a legitimation of Teresa's opinion of the Scardacciones: that they 'thought they were it just because they had money' (p.148). Just as his mother and aunt remain aloof from the rest of the village, Salvatore is a loner who looks for his own gain before thinking of others' misfortune.

Key point

Although Salvatore's betrayal appears to be an extension of his parents' snobbery, he ultimately makes peace with Michele and performs the crucial act of telling Michele that Filippo has been moved to Melichetti's. These reconciliatory actions suggest that although children are shaped by their parents' examples and instruction, they are not condemned to repeat their parents' mistakes. In this way, despite the bleakness of *I'm Not Scared*, the text always holds out hope for the future.

Images of the natural world

The third way in which the text repeatedly affirms the value of family bonds is through images of the natural world. The wasps building their nest even when Remo continually destroys it (p.175) and the owl circling above its concealed nest, reminding Michele of swallows 'wheeling round and round' if their nest is destroyed (pp.207–8), all speak for the natural integrity of family. For Michele, and for the text as a whole, the instinctively protective and nurturing impulse of parents in the world of animals sets the standard for human behaviour, thus exposing the behaviour of the village adults as unnatural, and fundamentally (not simply legally) wrong.

The image of the wasps building a nest in the shed is a central one, since it draws together several of the novel's important themes: the resilience of family bonds; the way that natural forces underpin social formations; the pleasure inherent in the perceptive observation of natural phenomena. It appears relatively late in the text, but its placement gives it extra significance, since it is counterposed to a series of human interactions in the preceding chapters that are characterised by conflict and dislocation. Of course, the reconciliation between Salvatore and Michele in the previous chapter speaks for a more positive, harmonious society, and the persistence of the wasps in building their nest suggest that such a society is underwritten by natural instincts.

Remo's wanton destruction of the nest, on the other hand, represents destructive impulses that threaten social, and especially family, structures. The image thus sharply defines the difference between Michele and Remo: one is a sensitive observer, appreciative of the natural world; the other is insensitive, determined to act upon the world for his own pleasure. Remo thus stands as a child-equivalent of Sergio, his attempt to destroy the wasps' nest a mirror-image of Sergio's casual squashing of a moth against the wall (p.166).

A final image of the integrity of family units in the animal world comes in the final pages, when Michele realises that the owl circling overhead is in fact hovering over her nest. He compares this behaviour to that of swallows that 'if you knock down their nest, keep wheeling round and round till they die of exhaustion' (pp.207–8). Once again, the nesting instinct is represented as an irrepressible force in the natural world, but one that has been corrupted in the human, social world.

The innocence of childhood

Childhood innocence, as embodied in Michele, is valued by the text in several ways. It is clearly precious because it can so easily be destroyed, shattered like the glass door Michele remembers breaking 'into a billion neat little cubes' (p.149). Once such innocence is shattered, it is unable to be restored, just as Michele's *absolute* trust in his father can never be recovered once he thinks to himself that 'Papa was the bogeyman' (p.87). Childhood innocence also, at its best, represents a way of negotiating the world that is inherently respectful, optimistic and sharing. Michele never questions the rightness of obtaining water and food for Filippo, of trying to keep his promises, of cleaning Filippo's face or conveying his mother's message of love to him.

Michele's narration presents everything in the novel – the natural world, children's games, the conflicts and ambitions of the adults – from his child's point of view. Not only is Michele innocent of doing any real harm (although he does cause a hen to be killed for no good reason), he also struggles to comprehend that others are as malicious and cruel as their actions reveal them to be. It is not that Michele is unfamiliar with violence: he is an acute observer of the natural world, familiar with its cycles of birth and death. Yet the violence carried out by the children's parents is of another order altogether, and seen from Michele's innocent perspective it seems all the more irrational and destructive.

If Michele represents the enlightened and compassionate aspects of childhood innocence, the text as a whole does not suggest that all children innately possess these qualities. Skull and Remo, in particular, display the negative, destructive attributes that, extended into adulthood, lead to the criminal activities of the Sergios and Felices of the world. To a certain extent they appear to have internalised these qualities from their upbringing, but their temperaments are so different from Michele's that part of their personalities seems due to nature, as much as nurture. Thus, *I'm Not Scared* presents a complex view of childhood, one which values its innocence but also resists an overly sentimental or idealistic portrayal of the child's-eye view of the world.

Natural order versus social disorder

michele frequently assesses his experiences against natural phenomena with which he is familiar. He likens Maria's devotion to himself to that of 'a little mongrel' (p.2); less flatteringly, Barbara scrambles 'like a demented sow' and 'swelled up like a turkey' (p.4). When he wonders whether the boy in the hole is dead or alive, he compares the apparent twitch of the arm with 'wasps, which keep on walking if you cut them in two' (p.30). As the narrative progresses, Michele becomes increasingly aware of the gap between the natural order of animals and plants, and the social order that adults have created and take part in; the latter often disregard the examples of the natural word before them to their own detriment.

Whereas Michele is a sensitive observer of the natural world, the adults shut themselves away in their houses, unable to see beyond their own frustrations. In order to 'buy' themselves a more comfortable existence, they embark on a plan of action that is not merely criminal, but that threatens to destroy everything worthwhile that they already possess. They lack, in other words, what Michele so abundantly has: a capacity to observe and appreciate the beauty and richness of the world they are actually in.

Moreover, Michele's perceptions of the natural world are full of moral lessons, examples of harmonious interactions between creatures and their environment. The image of the wasps persisting in making their nest despite the destructive actions of Remo has already been discussed. However, an additional point to make about this image is the significance of Michele recalling his father's answer to the question of how the wasps know what to do: "They just know. It's in their nature" (p.175). This reminds us of how Michele has always relied on his father as a source of knowledge and wisdom, in a way that he no longer can.

More significantly, Pino's response indicates that he too understands the strength and value of such natural forces, but has chosen to turn his back on them. Indeed, the kidnapping and cruel entrapment of Filippo – destroying the Carducci family unit – is directly analogous to Remo's wilful destruction of the wasps' nest.

Key point

The text repeatedly sets the natural world against the social one, suggesting that the adults have lost sight of the forces that underpin their own social fabric; forces that, if they opened up the shutters of their houses, they would see in action everywhere around them.

Harvesting nature

A powerful symbol of the tension between the adult, social world and the natural world is the combine harvester. At first, Michele compares the machine to the sea, but then it is likened to an animal, 'a huge metal grasshopper' (p.66). In this way, the narrative suggests that nature has been perverted by humans and turned into something monstrous; the human world, according to this image, acts rapaciously on the natural world, consuming and destroying it.

Of course, the harvesting of wheat brings money into the region, but for Michele at this time the machine evokes the hard, aggressive aspects of the human world. The harvester symbolises the human view of nature as a resource to be exploited, or – like Italo Natale's caged dogs in the ensuing image – an entity to be contained and confined (p.66). This is precisely what happens to the fields of wheat: they are eventually rendered lifeless packages, 'packed up in bales' by the roadside (p.177).

The power of storytelling

Throughout the novel, Michele's love of narrative conveys a strong message about the power of storytelling, and about the consequences when stories dry up. When conversations between himself and his father close down, with Michele unwilling to discuss where he rides during the day and Pino refusing to describe his travels in 'the North', they grow further apart, neither able to understand the motivations or values of the other. In contrast, Michele is captivated by the eccentric stories told by Filippo, featuring such exotic creatures as wash-bears and flying foxes, or casting the real word in a strange, other-worldly light: "The world's a place full of holes with dead people in them" (pp.109–10). Storytelling binds its participants together, just as silence as a response to a desire for knowledge drives people apart.

Imagining Tiger Jack

Another aspect of Michele's fascination with narrative is his rich imaginative life, inhabited by a cast of monsters, comic-book characters and biblical figures. At times, his internalisation of some of these stories generates fear where no basis for fear exists. The narrative actually draws our attention to the 'use' of fairytales in this respect, through Pino's advice that "Ghosts, werewolves and witches are just nonsense invented to frighten mugs like you" (p.49). In this sense, such stories prevent things from happening; they keep children in their place, obedient and compliant.

More importantly, though, the narrative suggests that stories have a very productive function, making affirmative actions possible in the face of oppression. Michele demonstrates this through his identification with the comic-book character Tiger Jack. This imaginative role-playing is effective because it allows Michele to place himself in the context of a narrative in which there is always a means of moving to the next point. Michele asks himself 'What would Tiger Jack do in my place?' when he first returns to the abandoned house and fears being caught by an ogre (p.44); on the final night, when his fears are even greater, he deploys the same tactic (p.201). Of course, Michele's actions of 'hopping like a bird' (p.44) or camouflaging himself (p.203) almost certainly have no real effect, but they are crucial to his ability to overcome his fear and move forward – still afraid, but nevertheless able to act.

This contrasts with the adults' attempt to overcome their own obstacles when the kidnapping plan goes awry. Unable to exchange Filippo for money, their captive becomes not an asset but a liability. Yet their attempt to negotiate this problem leads inexorably towards conflict and violence; as Michele observes, their own fear causes them to act like the 'green lizards', resorting to bluster and bravado rather than more productive, imaginative strategies. In a sense, we can say that the adults are stymied because they are unable to imagine themselves as part of a narrative, until Pino suggests a game that sets in train a meaningful series of actions.

QUESTIONS & ANSWERS

This section focuses on your own analytical writing on the text, and gives you strategies for producing high-quality responses in your coursework and exam essays.

Essay writing – an overview

An essay on a literary work is a formal and serious piece of writing that presents your point of view on the text, usually in response to a given topic. Your 'point of view' in an essay is your interpretation of the meaning of the text's language, structure, characters, situations and events, supported by detailed analysis of textual evidence.

Analyse – don't summarise

In your essays it is important to avoid simply summarising what happens in a text.

- A **summary** is a description or paraphrase (retelling in different words) of the characters and events. For example: 'Macbeth has a horrifying vision of a dagger dripping with blood before he goes to murder King Duncan.'
- An **analysis** is an explanation of the real meaning or significance that lies 'beneath' the text's words (and images, for a film). For example: 'Macbeth's vision of a bloody dagger shows how deeply uneasy he is about the violent act he is contemplating, and conveys his sense that supernatural forces are impelling him to act.'

A limited amount of summary is sometimes necessary to let your reader know which part of the text you wish to discuss. However, always keep this to a minimum and follow it immediately with your analysis of what this part of the text is really telling us.

Plan your essay

Carefully plan your essay so that you have a clear idea of what you are going to say. The plan ensures that your ideas flow logically, that your argument remains consistent and that you stay on the topic. An essay plan should be a list of **brief dot points** covering no more than half a page.

- Include your central argument or main contention – a concise statement of your overall response to the topic.
- Write down three or four dot points for each paragraph indicating the main idea and evidence/examples from the text. Note that in your essay you will need to *expand* on these points and *analyse* the evidence.

Structure your essay

An essay is a complete, self-contained piece of writing. It has a clear beginning (the introduction), middle (several body paragraphs) and end (the last paragraph or conclusion). It must also have a central argument that runs throughout, linking each paragraph to form a coherent whole.

The introduction establishes your overall response to the topic. It includes your main contention and outlines the main evidence you will refer to in the course of the essay. Write your introduction *after* you have done a plan and *before* you write the rest of the essay.

The body paragraphs argue your case – they present evidence from the text and explain how this evidence supports your argument. Each body paragraph needs:

- a strong **topic sentence** (usually the first sentence) that states the main point being made in the paragraph
- **evidence** from the text, including some brief quotations
- **analysis** of the textual evidence, with **explanation** of its significance and how it supports your argument

- **links back to the topic** in one or more statements, usually towards the end of the paragraph.

Connect the body paragraphs so that your discussion flows smoothly. Use some linking words and phrases such as 'similarly' and 'on the other hand', though don't start every paragraph like this. Another strategy is to use a significant word from the last sentence of one paragraph in the first sentence of the next.

Use key terms from the topic – or synonyms for them – throughout, so the relevance of your discussion to the topic is always clear.

The conclusion ties everything together and finishes the essay. It includes strong statements that emphasise your central argument and provide a clear response to the topic.

Avoid simply restating the points made earlier in the essay – this will end on a very flat note and imply that you have run out of ideas and vocabulary. The conclusion should be a logical extension of what you have written, not just a repetition or summary of it. Writing an effective conclusion can be a challenge. Try using these tips:

- Start by linking back to the final sentence of the second-last paragraph – this helps your writing to flow, rather than leaping back to your main contention straight away.
- Use synonyms and expressions with equivalent meanings to vary your vocabulary. This allows you to reinforce your line of argument without being repetitive.
- When planning your essay, think of one or two broad statements or observations about the text's wider meaning. These should be related to the topic and your overall argument. Keep them for the conclusion, since they will give you something 'new' to say but still follow logically from your discussion. The introduction will be focused on the topic, but the conclusion can present a wider view of the text.

Essay topics

1 "I must pluck up courage and look."

'Although Michele experiences fear, he never lets his fear override his moral convictions.' Discuss.

2 'Although Michele is devastated by the betrayals of family and friends, he never stops trusting in human goodness.' Discuss.

3 'Michele learns that loyalty and trust are far more valuable than money or objects.' Do you agree?

4 "Why did those wasps make the nest?" How do images of nature contrast with, and expose, the flawed family relationships in *I'm Not Scared*?

5 Why does Michele continue to love and respect his father, despite knowing what his father has done and is prepared to do?

6 '*I'm Not Scared* suggests that there is a form of wisdom in childhood innocence that adults ignore at their peril.' Do you agree?

7 '*I'm Not Scared* shows that there is nothing wrong with being scared – it's knowing what's right that is important.' Discuss.

8 '*I'm Not Scared* shows that even the most tightly-knit community can be split by individual greed and self-interest.' Discuss.

9 '*I'm Not Scared* explores the consequences for innocent people when desperate people dispense with moral codes of conduct.' Discuss.

10 'Human compassion towards the helpless and vulnerable is shown to be frighteningly shallow in *I'm Not Scared*.' Do you agree?

Analysing a sample topic

7 ***'I'm Not Scared* shows that there is nothing wrong with being scared – it's knowing what's right that is important.' Discuss.**

The underlying idea in this topic is that people's fear can stop them from behaving appropriately, an ethical dilemma that Michele faces repeatedly throughout the narrative.

Consider the following points that support the contention:

- As the title suggests, the characters tend to say 'I'm not scared', but in fact they often *are* scared. Thus, the title is ironic, and hints at the characters' tendency to bluff, to hide vulnerability behind a bold exterior.

- Note the image of 'the spitting of the green lizards' (p.189). Michele understands why the adults are acting like this, but he also knows that such responses to fear are short-term defences only.

- Michele knows that sometimes he must put his fear aside because there is a moral imperative to act. This occurs, trivially, at the very start: his fear of coming last in the race is less important than his obligation to help Maria. Later he helps Filippo, despite his fear of the consequences.

- Other characters try to deny that they are scared, but compared to Michele their sense of right and wrong is more affected by their fear. Felice is taunted by Sergio for saying "I'm not scared" (p.193) in relation to killing Filippo, when he clearly is scared.

- Pino and Sergio show no fear, but they also seem the most callous of the adults, the most prepared to compromise what they think is morally right in order to obtain what they want.

The above points support the contention, since in each case fear is an understandable emotion, but how each character values their moral beliefs as opposed to their prospects for material gain is the basis of how we view them (as good or bad people, generous or selfish, and so on).

In conclusion, you could say that the novel expresses hope that we will remain true to our moral convictions even when faced with danger and gripped by fear.

Disagreeing with this contention

Disagreeing with the contention would be difficult in this instance, but it is worth thinking about how it might be done in order to introduce more complexity into your argument. As the above comment on the conclusion shows, straightforward agreement with the contention can lead to a one-dimensional essay which tends simply to *repeat* itself over and over, rather than *developing* its argument. To achieve this kind of complexity in your essay, try to develop a position of qualified agreement with the contention; that is, agreement with some exceptions.

How would you argue that the novel is on the side of the kidnappers rather than Michele? At first it seems impossible to sustain such an argument. However, you could generate a more complex response to the question by distinguishing between different kinds of fear, or different layers of 'right' and 'wrong', in order to demonstrate your understanding of the text's complexities. And Ammaniti does, on the whole, suggest that there are two sides to each situation, that there may be more than one valid view of what is 'right' at any given moment.

For instance:

- Michele seems as frightened of imaginary creatures as of real men; this fear does not help him act in the real world, and in fact to some extent his childish beliefs blind him to the real motivations and actions of men. So, whether it's wrong to be scared depends on what is being feared and what one's responsibilities are.

- Michele does act compassionately, but there is also an element of selfish possessiveness in his attitude to Filippo: initially he keeps his knowledge a secret simply because 'He was mine. He was my secret discovery' (p.30), regardless of the consequences for the boy lying in the hole.
- Pino and Teresa are protective of their children, and they know that Filippo's kidnapping is 'wrong'; yet they also have a sense of the social injustice of their place in the world.
- This hints at a moral universe that is more complex and ambiguous than that which Michele can grasp. In this light, Pino's claim that "The world's wrong" (p.157) reflects not so much his inability to know right from wrong, but a very different experience of and perspective on the world than Michele has. The text thus suggests that 'knowing what's right' is not always straightforward.

You might conclude that the text does not condemn those who are afraid, but shows that knowing what to be afraid of is crucial to one's moral judgement, and thus to effective action in the world. Or, that *I'm Not Scared* shows the value of adhering to a moral code despite one's fears, but that deciding what is right and wrong in any situation might be more complicated than it appears through the eyes of an intelligent, but naive, child.

SAMPLE ANSWER

***'I'm Not Scared* demonstrates that fear becomes an undermining emotion when terrible secrets are kept.' Discuss.**

Fear, and the reactions of characters to it, is a central theme in Niccolò Ammaniti's *I'm Not Scared*. Michele Amitrano's frightened reaction to the kidnapped boy, Filippo, is augmented by the nightmares and visions he is haunted by, and the keeping of this secret undermines Michele's ability and desire to help Filippo. In addition, the adults' clandestine activities cause disharmony and quarrelling that damages the close-knit relationships of the village and, potentially, the safety of the citizens.

Though Michele's initial reaction to the 'dead' boy is one of curiosity, the dread caused by his secret begins to manifest itself in nightmares and visions. Michele wakes, sweating, from a dream in which Lazarus rises up and attacks Jesus, saying, 'leave the dead alone ... with blood smeared lips'. That same night, he envisions Filippo 'dead in the earth ... worms coming out of his blue lips'. Michele's fear initially prevents him from assisting Filippo in any way, believing him to be a 'monster ... a werewolf'. Michele refers often to supernatural beings and folktales, his fear of them often interrupting his sleep and his actions – 'They would just be waiting for me to fall asleep'; 'they would rise up ... and bury [Filippo]'. Furthermore, this trepidation is amplified by his identification of his father as 'the bogeyman ... by day ... good, but at night ... bad'. The likening of his father to a monster both diminishes Michele's ability to interact with his father and undermines the relationship between them. The secret Papa is keeping causes Michele to question his father's nature, and this is the primary cause of the fear that serves to weaken their relationship.

The boy who is the subject of the secret, Filippo, is distressed by fear. He raves incoherently about 'the little wash-bears' and his 'guardian angel'. The boy becomes not only physically destabilised by terror, but also emotionally volatile, shrieking over and over the question, 'Am I dead?' Filippo becomes so overcome with fright and anguish that he makes no effort to escape, even when it is safe to, 'kneeling under the blanket ... in the same position [Michele] had left him'. Psychologically, he retreats further into himself, crying, 'My mother's dead ... And papa's dead ... They're all dead'. Further, when Michele offers to take him out of the hole Filippo hides away, saying, 'Outside there's no air ... I'll suffocate. I don't want to go out there'. He is clearly debilitated by his fears when the truth about his circumstances is kept from him.

The hindering emotion of fear is also evident in the actions and interactions of the adults of Acqua Traverse. The kidnapping plot they are involved in is the product of desperation, as shown by Michele's father, who asks, 'didn't you want to go away from [here]?' The adults' fear is evident throughout the novel. Their constant arguing and the disarray of Michele's house imply they are in a dire situation, their apprehension undermining their ability to work cooperatively and effectively. The grilling Papa gives Michele regarding his dealings with Filippo emphasises how grave the situation has become, and when he speaks of the others shooting Filippo in the head, the implication is that Michele and the rest of the village are in potential physical danger as a result of the adults' actions. Papa substitutes the pronoun 'him' for Filippo's name, showing how he has had to distance himself from and dehumanise the boy in order to go through with the kidnapping. His fear is palpable, and it is evident that his ability to react normally to any situation is deteriorating as a result.

The physical restraints placed upon the citizens of Acqua Traverse are manifestations of fear. So, too, are the apparent role reversals of the adults within the village. Felice tends to react aggressively to the orders of the adults, but when Sergio chastises him for going down to the sea, Felice responds by merely complaining about the old man to Michele, threatening the former only while he is not present. The impression one receives of Felice is of a belligerent, independent youth, yet Barbara's mother chastises him and his father cuffs him around the head like a child. A similar incident occurs when Sergio calls Papa an imbecile. The lack of response of these erstwhile authoritative characters to these insults demonstrates the shifting social hierarchy within the village due to the adults' dread and trepidation.

Thus, *I'm Not Scared* dramatically illustrates the undermining power of fear in the presence of secrets. It is manifest in the nightmares of Michele and in the deteriorating relationship between Michele and his father. It is also evident in Filippo's physical and emotional debilitation, as well as in the volatile interactions and the shifting social hierarchy of the adults of Acqua Traverse. When terrible secrets are kept, such as the kidnapping of Filippo, fear weakens family relationships, destroys community cohesion and leads to tragedy.

REFERENCES & READING

Text

Ammaniti, Niccolò, *I'm Not Scared*, translated by Jonathan Hunt, Text Publishing, Melbourne, 2003. First published as *Io non ho paura*, Giulio Einaudi Editore, 2001.

Websites

http://ehlt.flinders.edu.au/deptlang/fulgor/volume1i3/papers/fulgor_v1i3_Book_reviews.htm

An interesting review including background material on Niccolò Ammaniti by Dr Diana Glenn.

http://ercoleguidi.altervista.org/anthology/ammaniti.htm

The novel's opening in Italian and English side by side; the English translation is slightly different from Jonathan Hunt's which makes for an interesting comparison.

Acknowledgement

The author gratefully acknowledges the contribution of Gemma van Cuylenburg of Newhaven College in translating Italian terms and phrases for this text guide.